Praise for Direct Hit

"For all those pastors, preachers and 'wanna-be' church leaders who deeply desire to make a difference for Christ, this is the ministry book to read. Paul Borden does a fantastic job of laying out what needs to be done in the 21st century church as well as showing us exactly how to do it. If you need some hands-on help as well as some spiritual stimulation to get your parish off the dime, *Direct Hit* is for you!"

—Scott A. Wenig, Chair
The Division of Christian Ministries, Denver Seminary
Lead Pastor, Aspen Grove Community Church, Littleton, CO

* *

"Transformational change, both personal and corporate, is the need of the hour. In *Direct Hit*, Paul Borden takes aim at this crucial issue to help leaders wrestle with the key tools to help their organizations grow to the next level."

—Dave Travis, Executive Vice President
Leadership Network

* *

"*Direct Hit* and its predecessor, *Hit the Bullseye*, have been a long time in coming to the church, but thank God they are here! *Hit the Bullseye* redirected the church to the mission field around us, while *Direct Hit* thrusts Christians on to leadership in the mission field in order to affect change of individuals and entire communities. Most pastors and churches are looking for ways to revitalize their churches. Paul Borden has boldly stepped into this arena with solid, proven principles of ministry. Every church leader needs not only to read this book but also to study it well for successful church leadership."

—Rev. Dr. Lawrence Wilkes, Dean
Robert Schuller School for Preaching

* *

"*Direct Hit* should be required reading for every pastor in America, and it should be re-read every six months! It's the best I've seen on what kind of specific senior leadership is required to transform church decline into congregational vitality."

—Sue Nilson Kibbey, Executive Pastor
Ginghamsburg Church

"Here are refreshing words of hope for churches that have stagnated and for the people who desire to lead them through the painful but rewarding process of revitalization. As a sage and practitioner, Paul presents a biblically-laced fabric, woven with the threads of vision, mission, urgency, strategy, and tactics. His compelling call is to those whose passion will carry them forward for the cause of Jesus Christ."

—Stephen LeBar, Ph.D., Executive Director
Conservative Baptists of America

* *

"If you want to remain in a church that is discouragingly ineffectual, dysfunctional, and certain only of its eventual demise, this book not is not for you. But if you want to know how to develop new vision, passion, and reproductive growth, then read this book now!"

—Dr. Stuart Robinson, Senior Pastor
Crossway Baptist Church, Burwood East, Victoria, Australia

* *

"Paul Borden, a skilled physician of the soul, offers a thorough and dynamic process for understanding the local church. He courageously assists in uncovering the roadblocks to health and growth by asking the difficult questions with rare precision. As a superintendent of churches using his tools, I see the fruit of renewed congregations that emerge."

—Thomas F. Tumblin, Ph.D., Associate Professor of Leadership
Asbury Theological Seminary

* *

"Church leaders need more than motivation and inspiration. Paul Borden explains *how* to change dysfunction to health and decline to growth."

—Leith Anderson, Senior Pastor
Wooddale Church, Eden Prairie, MN

* *

"*Direct Hit* gets to the heart of the matter. Pastors—it's about Christ and leadership! Congregation—it's about Christ's purpose and mission! There is plenty of interpretation and coaching here for both sides of the pastoral relationship, but above all there is urgency. It's time to stop dithering and get on with it!"

—Tom Bandy, President
Easum, Bandy, and Associates

Direct Hit
Aiming Real Leaders
at the Mission Field

Paul D. Borden

Abingdon Press
Nashville

DIRECT HIT: AIMING REAL LEADERS AT THE MISSION FIELD

Copyright © 2006 Paul D. Borden
All rights reserved.

This book is printed on acid-free, recycled, elemental-chlorine-free paper.

Library of Congress Cataloging-in-Publication Data

Borden, Paul D.
  Direct hit : aiming real leaders at the mission field / Paul D. Borden.
    p. cm.
  ISBN-13: 978-0-687-33194-9
  ISBN-10: 0-687-33194-3
  1. Church renewal. 2. Church growth. 3. Change--Religious aspects--Christianity. 4. Change (Psychology)--Religious aspects--Christianity. I. Title.

  BV600.B66 2006
  253--dc22

                                                                2006021663

Scripture quotations, unless otherwise indicated, are from the *New Revised Standard Version of the Bible*, copyright © 1989, by the Division of Christian Education of the National Council of the Churches of Christ in the United States of America. Used by permission. All rights reserved.

06 07 08 09 10 11 12 13 14 15—10 09 08 07 06 05 04 03 02

MANUFACTURED IN THE UNITED STATES OF AMERICA

Contents

Direct Hit
is dedicated to:

LaShelle and Wren
Jeff, Keena, and Jackson
Luke, Kelli, Emma, and Megan

with a reverent heavenly nod to:

Cory

Your Love Encourages Me
Your Support Motivates Me
Your Care Comforts Me

Teresa, your intelligence, wit, insight, and
passion continue to motivate me.
Your love and confidence in me keeps me going.
This book was written in large measure because of you.

Acknowledgements

Pastors, spouses, mentors, coaches, church planters, intentional interims, lay leaders, prayer teams, and region board members in the healthy growing congregations of GHC—You are the reason any books have been written about our region. I honor you. Thank you for your ministry, your character, and your willingness to stand tall for our God and for God's mission. YOU ARE THE BEST!

Pam, David, JD, Bill, and Pablo—Wow! You make my job a joy. Thanks for all you do to advance the kingdom of God.

Conrad—God used you to start a fire in GHC. Thanks for your vision, courage, and leadership. Thanks for setting things up for great success.

Richard, Connie, Bud, Dan, Raul, Tom, Heather, Michelle, Susan, Marge, Judy, and Larry—Thanks for all you do to make the rest of us look so good in our ministries.

Haddon and Frank—Thanks for investing in me and in my ministry and for being the human instruments for any success I experience.

Leith—You were a friend to someone in need, and you remain a dear friend who constantly teaches me new ideas and paradigms whenever I am around you.

Dennis, Terry, Evan, Ray, Elmer, Bill C., Pat, and Bill H.—You have been friends and mentors who have been there for me during both good times and bad times. Thanks!

John, Mike, James, Scott, Nick, and Tim—Thanks for allowing me to invade your lives. Your ministries are a joy to me.

Allan, Helen, Stuart, John, Brian, Murray R. and Murray C.—You are my alien friends and colleagues in ministry around the world. You model God's grace in effective ministry. Thank you for encouraging me.

Mal, Art, and Bill—You modeled ministry for me early on. Mal and Bev—You were there when I was ready to quit a long time ago.

Tom—Thanks for all your invaluable advice in creating *Hit the Bullseye*. Also, thanks for all your personal encouragement to me and to our region. You are a true colleague in ministry.

Paul—You and the team at Abingdon always make what I write look so much better than it is. Your gifts and talents amaze me. Thanks for your ministry to me and to the readers.

Foreword

Paul Borden has had the church in his sights for some time now. Through a couple of decades, he has consulted with pastors, congregations, and judicatories. He has prodded us, challenged us, penetratingly criticized us, and then inspired us to grow healthier congregations. He not only fired off periodic salvos at us, but he also got down in the trenches with us and, in the heat of battle, thereby renewed a large part of an entire denomination. In Paul's last book, *Hit the Bullseye* (©2003, Abingdon Press), he put together all that knowledge and experience and took aim at the church, particularly the declining, aging, self-absorbed North American church and its pastors. Now, in the book before us, Paul scores a "direct hit."

Take cover—all you pastors and church leaders who have been making alibis, dodging the numbers, defending our decline, and excusing our infidelities. In this little book, Borden has packed just about everything he has learned from his decades of efforts to lead a renewal of the church. All of this firepower is delivered in a direct, focused, and essential guide that challenges churches either to reenlist in Christ's mission to get back the world or else get out of his way. We can duck, but we can't forever hide.

Paul provocatively chooses a martial metaphor for the title of his book. I think he does this because Paul believes that if we're in mission with Jesus, the Prince of Peace, we are in a kind of war. Jesus casts fire on the earth that produces an incendiary fellowship of those who have the guts to be in mission with the living Christ. Through ordinary people like us, that mission spreads like a wildfire across the earth. But nothing catches fire without leaders— those who are willing to go where Jesus orders us to go and to speak what Jesus commands us to say. So Jesus' question is rarely, "Do you agree?" but more typically, "Will you join up and head toward the front lines?"

I recently read an article in *The Christian Century* by a seminary professor who gave the standard defense against church mission strategists like Borden. After years of teaching at a seminary that—like many of our seminaries—somehow teaches students how to kill churches rather than how to grow them, this professor once again trotted out the old "I'd rather be faithful than successful" argument in an attempt to deflect a direct hit from some wild-eyed fanatic like Paul. I wondered what St. Luke or St. Paul, or for that matter the entire New Testament, would make of the professor's argument that gradual, boring death and decline—accompanied by the loss of generations of would-be Christians and a morbid shrinkage of mission efforts—is a sure sign of real faithfulness.

I feel sure that Paul Borden would read the professor's comments and say, "Now do you see why mainline Protestantism is headed for the morgue?"

Borden unashamedly calls us pastors and church leaders (I have heard him be ruthless on bishops and seminary profs like me) back to strong, visionary leadership that boldly measures fidelity to Jesus in terms of effectiveness, results, passion, success in reaching the lost, and, yes, results measured in numbers. Jesus makes things grow and loves to raise the dead. Anybody who is faithful to him will do the same, leaving the dead to bury their dead. If God had asked Paul to write a book of the New Testament, rather than *Direct Hit,* I think he would have written the *Acts of the Apostles.*

Although most of the theology behind Paul's thoughts on Christian leadership is assumed rather than demonstrated, I detect a vibrant faith in the living, speaking God; the relentless work of the Holy Spirit; and a loving determination of Jesus Christ to use us to get back what belongs to him. Paul is a master in stressing the practical, specific implications of his convictions about leadership for a growing church and has this ruthless, single-minded attachment to the mission of Christ above all else.

Paul can be a royal pain in the neck for church bureaucrats like me who too easily settle for too little in Christ's church. So I confess that there's part of me that wishes Paul had not scored such a direct hit in this book. Now the bishop in Birmingham who lamented, "How on earth can we find a way out of our current malaise?" is forced to ask, "Am I going to get passionate about the mission of Jesus or stand around just keeping house as the place falls in?"

Nothing is urged in these pages that hasn't been tested and found absolutely essential. Everything here is pared down to the one thing needful. The book moves us to a new vision of church leadership, indeed, a fresh sense of a church that is, in the power of the Holy Spirit, relentlessly turned out toward the world in the name of Jesus. With radical passion and a masterful grasp of what is absolutely necessary if the leadership of the church is to move beyond mere maintenance toward real mission, Paul tells us how to do it. He not only ruthlessly attacks the introversion, denial, and depression that infect too many pastors and their congregations, but he also moves on to practical steps that we can take if we would share in Jesus' exciting future. He tells us what to do and how to do it, lest we attempt to weasel out of the mission.

I predict this book will either change the whole way you think about your God-given ministry or else you will be forced to burn it before you finish it, so strong are its arguments, so focused is its message, so direct is its hit.

Like I said, Paul Borden can be a real pain in the neck. For Jesus' sake.

Will Willimon, Bishop
The North Alabama Conference of the United Methodist Church

CHAPTER ONE
It's More Than Just Talk

The cultural currency of the ecclesiastical world is words. For humans, it began when God created the first people and spoke to them. God continued to speak throughout history and saw to it that the words were shared, remembered, and recorded.

God then sent THE WORD, who became flesh and dwelt among us. THE WORD, Jesus Christ, conducted his ministry while speaking in all kinds of settings to a variety of people who congregated with him. Whether from one-on-one interviews or from preaching to thousands, his words were remembered. The words and deeds of Jesus and the apostles were remembered and revealed to future generations of believers.

For nearly two thousand years, the followers of Jesus have spent time communicating the thoughts of God accurately and inaccurately in sermons, teachings, writings, prayers, stories, poems, hymns, and songs, and through the endless making of books.

As a result of all this remembering, revealing, and interpreting, most of what is done in congregations, missions, and ministries depends primarily on written and spoken communication. We pray, preach, share, testify, witness, sing, quote, print, e-mail, type, teach, and read words that convey an extensive variety of pious and divine thoughts.

Therefore, we usually expect that for one to lead well in a congregation, he or she must have the ability to communicate reasonably well in some form so that people are motivated to follow.

Our expectation for strong leadership is not being met in most places. This is one major reason why the Church in the Western world is deeply in need of change. Renewal that refocuses believers and congregations on seriously communicating the Great Commission is perhaps the greatest priority facing the Church. Leaders desiring to drive such systemic change must understand that this endeavor demands the strategic use of words. The majority of change agents in a congregation will be leaders who have a plan for change that includes a major overhaul of communication strategy.

Let's take pastors as an example. Too many former pastors are now selling insurance and funeral plans because they wanted to lead change but failed in communicating well the changes they were attempting to implement. They failed in large measure because they had no communication strategy. Probably no profession other than pastor has such a vast opportunity to lead change through individual and group communication. My hunch is that many executives in large corporations, non-profits, small businesses, sales, or even politics would be envious of the opportunities pastors have for leading change.

Each week people come and sit voluntarily so the pastor, whose salary they pay, can speak to them. Although different traditions circumscribe the time allotted for this communication, pastors have from ten to forty minutes or more to talk and communicate with congregants. And in most traditions the pastor is given time either before or after the formal presentation to make comments to the audience. Perhaps the only other leaders who have such access to their followers are coaches of sports teams or conductors of symphonies.

Furthermore, every time there is a meeting of the congregation, the pastor usually can take time to speak or is given time to communicate. This opportunity is afforded not only in informal gatherings but also in meetings where major decisions are made about the future direction of the congregation.

In addition to the public visibility, pastors are paid to spend time in study. This time for research provides pastors with the opportunity to examine key issues related to change, and to develop strategies and tactics to enhance the process and speed of change. Even in some rural settings where pastors are expected to be out and about talking with the community, such interaction gives the pastor insight into people and situations, while allowing the pastor to "test the waters" about changes that may be pursued in the future.

In most congregations, people are willing to meet with the pastor when she or he asks. These meetings enable the pastor to develop relationships, model discipleship, and train leaders who may be open to following when change is being implemented.

All that is true for pastors, except for the weekly task of preaching, is true for congregational staff members. Not only do they have access to people, who often allow them to intrude on their schedules, but they also are usually given the opportunity to speak at every meeting they attend.

Lay leaders in congregations have the same access to leaders and other laity that pastors have. They are often involved in meetings where they are expected and given time to speak. They may be put in charge of groups where they are expected to lead. Any leadership they exert is generally through oral or written communication. The culture of most congregations allows them to call and make appointments with people, most of whom are willing to meet.

All of these relationships are possible because the cultural currency of the Church is words. No other social entity in our culture allows and expects people to communicate with others as often and as regularly as occurs in the world of a congregation.

Yet despite all the opportunities to influence others for change, most congregations and the Church in general are declining and moving more and more inward (focusing on themselves) as each day passes.

There are multiple reasons for this inward direction that the Church is taking, but *Direct Hit* will address two major ones. The first is that many people in leadership positions in congregations either are not willing to lead transformational change or do not even see themselves as leaders. The second reason for decline is that even when people assume the role of leader and lead transformational change, they often do not have a well-developed communication strategy to affect such change.

Now it is true that only God produces real change, and only God grows the Church. However, it is also true that God usually works through leaders who function wisely and are committed to God. The Scripture is filled with stories of leaders who came to the people of God when they, like the Church, had lost hope and were convinced nothing could change. However, when those leaders led well, God brought all kinds of transformational changes as a result of their wisdom and effective communication. The good news is that I have not only seen God do this for the people in the Scriptures; God has done it for our part of the Church too.

Hope

In 1997, I, along with others, began working with a group of over two hundred congregations in northern California and northwest Nevada, affiliated with the American Baptist Churches of the West. From 1997 to 2001, we experienced a miracle of God. In 1997, less than 20 percent of these congregations were growing. Many had experienced growth and health in the 1950s and '60s, gathering over five hundred in worship each Sunday. By the time we arrived, many had less than one hundred in worship attendance and the congregations were aging, often with few if any younger families attending. However, by 2001, over 70 percent were growing, and many of those congregations today are averaging between three hundred and nine hundred people in worship attendance. Today we are aggressively planting new large congregations that launch with over three hundred people in worship. Our miracle continues.

God used several major human factors to produce this miracle in this part of the Church. The first key factor is that our change began as we focused on the crucial role of leadership and made it a value in our congregations. Usually we started with our pastors. For those who were here before 1997 and are still here, now leading much larger congregations, it required a significant spiritual and mental shift in how they viewed their role. It was a role that took some convincing prior to acceptance, and then required intensive training and mentoring to fulfill. But as pastors have accepted this role, they have experienced a dynamic change both personally and professionally.

However, not only pastors need to become leaders. Good leaders are constantly raising up new leaders. The pastors in our region understand that one of their primary responsibilities is to develop their staff and board members as leaders. As our congregations grow, more and more staff members are recruited, mostly raised up from the congregations they attend. For example, we now have a pastoral cluster designed for female full-time staff members, which is led by a female staff member. Most of the women in this cluster were not in church leadership five to ten years ago. A congregation grows in proportion to the number of new leaders that are being developed every year.

We now have board members who not only protect and cheer their pastor as she or he leads; they too lead. These new leaders are active in a governance model that allows mission and vision to be achieved. However, they are also learning that their most important function is not sitting on a board but leading an effective ministry in the congregation. We now have board members who are invited to go outside our region and denomination to help other pastors, lay leaders, and congregations make transformational changes.

My work with congregations and denominations for thirty years around the world has demonstrated over and over again what others continue to say about all organizations, religious or secular. The ability for any organization to effectively accomplish its purpose is ultimately determined by leaders who are effective because they communicate well. Effective congregations—defined by the ability to fulfill the Great Commission—have outstanding leaders. This is true for new church plants, growing congregations, or congregations who desperately need transformation. Some might say that this principle is self-evident, but with so many dying and ineffective churches, is it really obvious to everyone that the leader is the key?

The good news we have discovered in our part of the kingdom (and what I have discovered around the world) is that many pastors who never saw themselves as leaders are willing to take on that role and with training and mentoring are now able to lead healthy, growing, reproducing ministries. These pastors are becoming adept at developing other disciples as leaders too. Many of our congregations are developing a leadership community that is constantly growing and producing new leaders.

Barriers to Leading Change

#1 The first barrier has already been stated: Most pastors do not see themselves as the leaders of congregations, except perhaps when accepting the title of "spiritual leader." Few pastors are willing to assume the role of a leader who takes responsibility for mobilizing the congregation to accept the mission of obeying our Lord's Great Commission: to make disciples for Jesus. Instead, many pastors and other church staff presume that their job is to call individuals to personal discipleship. This assumption permits them to take on roles as the congregation's chaplain, preacher, theologian, disciple-maker, and so forth. These roles are validated by the pastor's training and the expectations of the congregation. However, the idea of leading a community of people (a local congregation) to fulfill a mission and achieve a vision is foreign to their way of thinking. It is not part of their paradigm.

#2 A second barrier is that pastors have been trained and often perform in an environment where faithful endeavor is honored, but fruitful results are not expected or demanded. This avoidance of results is present not only for pastors but also for any individual who possesses ministry responsibilities in the congregation. And so we have declining congregations and declining denominations. The Church shies away from accountability perhaps better than any other organization in our society. The incentive to change is particularly absent when the ministry environment reacts so negatively and often labels change as unspiritual.

Serving in a world where a "slow, painful death" is the norm frustrates many pastors and lay leaders. However, there are so few models and systems from which to gain encouragement and experience that these people do not know what to do, and they are without hope. Too often they attend conferences where stories of health and growth motivate them to return to their congregation with great excitement, only to have that excitement drowned with the discouragement of working within a system that is so highly dysfunctional that it vacuums any joy or excitement from the soul.

A third barrier to change is that many congregations are led by a handful of people who have gained that position by default. A long line of ineffectual pastors coupled with the continual loss of key lay leaders has defaulted into these people taking over control of the congregation. Though often they often start with good motivations, their leadership deteriorates to one of conserving the status quo. Their fear of losing more people, coupled with an introverted theology that the congregation exists for them and those like them, causes them to gain personal significance from holding things together. The thought of risk and acting in faith scares them because it threatens their security and significance, which motivates them to resist any change that tampers with their influence and control. The result is a strong and often organized passive-aggressive attack against any leader who wants the congregation to become active in fulfilling the Great Commission. The people in control realize that a great influx of new people would mean a loss of control and that such a loss would be accompanied with a decline in their own status. Therefore, they attempt to lead with negative communication, sometimes even scaring off new people before they can become part of the congregation.

The last major barrier is the polity of most congregations. Regardless of the denomination and its polity, most congregations in the United States are designed to be small, remain small, and function ineffectively in the twenty-first century. These structures, from their inception until now, reflect the cultures in which they were created. Unlike in the Scriptures, authority is divided from responsibility to act. There is little if any accountability for results, and the little that does exist is not applied with consistency throughout the system. In some cases, triangulation is codified into the system. Egalitarianism is honored over effectiveness, and bold leadership is greatly discouraged. Change always starts with mission and vision. However, no new mission and vision will take hold and last over time if the structure is not changed to allow both to flourish. The bureaucratic structures of our congregations do not produce leaders or allow leaders to lead, and such structures usually drive off the good or strong leaders at both the clergy and lay levels.

The good news is that we have seen God break through these barriers in many of our congregations, as well as in congregations all over the globe. It is important to note that God used leaders who had clear communication strategies to produce such miracles. While it is true that in some cases God worked in spite of us, in most cases God worked through leaders who took responsibility for results, were strategic in developing the right tactics, and communicated in such a way that these strategies and tactics could be employed effectively.

Factors in Leading Change

Effective congregations are led by pastors and a team of leaders who are clear about their mission and focused on achieving a vision. Unlike the majority of congregations that are either on a plateau or declining, effective congregations are healthy, growing, committed to reproduction, and open to changes that will move them from one level of effectiveness to the next. The constantly changing culture, wherein what is new today is passé tomorrow, demands fluidity in strategies, tactics, and methods. Healthy congregations are outward-focused, and they maintain that focus against tremendous forces that are constantly encouraging an inward bent. Such congregations are led by leaders who regularly implement change. Such leaders create an environment where change becomes the norm and maintaining the status quo is unacceptable.

Many pastors have gladly accepted the role of leading individuals to change. The role of leading someone to move away from a destructive and sinful life to embrace Jesus Christ and his teaching is what has often motivated pastors to choose their profession over others. However, few pastors have taken seriously the role of leading an entire congregation to change from conducting ministry for personal consumption to conducting ministry for the purpose of transforming the community that surrounds it. Those who do take on this more biblical and global role have not been trained to do so, and there is often little help in pursuing this role from either their peers or the denominations in which they find fellowship.

One major assumption of *Direct Hit* is that congregations are created by God to be God's primary tool for making individual disciples and for changing entire communities. God expects local churches to take on the stewardship of changing the social and political structures of their communities, primarily through the evangelism of individuals and then by helping these individuals live out their new lives together in Christ as they work to bring near the kingdom of God. If this is so, then the pastor's primary leadership responsibility under God is directed more to the congregation as an entity than it is to the individuals who comprise the congregation. Such a stewardship only happens as pastors act as transformational leaders, developing and surrounding themselves with other transformational leaders.

[handwritten margin note: Corporate vs. indiv. paradigm]

The following chapters will focus on the role of leaders in communicating a change strategy to achieve the goal that God has set before them. There are a number of books about what leaders ought to be and what they ought to do. However, little has been said or written about how leaders communicate with followers to achieve grand visions. The scope of *Direct Hit* will go far beyond the formal communication events that leaders are expected to present, such as sermons or teaching events. A more comprehensive communication strategy places these formal communication events as only one piece of a complex agenda for change.

The Role of Communication for Jesus

The primary skill required for strong leadership in the church is the ability to use words. Behavior is important, and one whose behavior is inconsistent with his or her words is not only a hypocrite but also will eventually fail as a leader.

Outstanding leaders understand that they have signed up for a 24/7 task. Every spoken word, every phone call, every e-mail, every verbal interaction (formal or informal) with people in the congregation reflects an overall communication strategy for change. If we lead change only through formal presentations or meetings, then we have unclear thinking about the nature of the task. Every venue, every day—no matter how seemingly insignificant—ought to be a specific tactic in our overall communication strategy. Leaders cannot afford to have throw away conversations. The skill is not found only in the words. The quality is found in the intonation, the body language, the eye contact, and more, when helping people see we are excited about a new vision.

Our model for this communication is Jesus Christ. He was never off message from the first communication recorded about him until his return to the Father. He understood that all his words were crucial for the task at hand. When a frantic Mary and Joseph finally find him in the Temple at age twelve, interacting with religious leaders rather than apologizing for being lost, he reminded them that he is about his father's business.

Jesus then told John the Baptist that John must baptize him, not the other way around. He confronted Nicodemus about how the Old Testament spoke of him and the need for spiritual birth. He would not let the woman at the well use excuses and religious arguments to distract him from making his point. He comforted his disciples when they were confused and confronted them when they were proud. He attacked the religious leaders who would deny his claims while speaking kindly and gently to those who were denied status by the culture. He forgave those who killed him shortly after pronouncing judgment on those who had rejected him. Following his resurrection, Jesus commanded his followers to make disciples while informing them of the coming Holy Spirit. Every word Jesus spoke had purpose. Jesus had a mission to fulfill, and he understood that his communication with people in the short time he was on earth must be used wisely.

While the Gospel writers shared only a small portion of Jesus' words and behaviors—during the normal events of life, he probably had some banal conversations—the writers clearly demonstrate that Jesus, when acting as a leader, was always on target with his words.

Even though he preached sermons and gave discourses, Jesus is primarily known for telling stories. Most people understand best when communication is concrete, not abstract or obtuse. Jesus also recognized that stories need not be explained to be understood. Often the story has so involved the listeners that they can understand the point without further explanation. As a great leader, Jesus communicated in ways that caused people to listen. Stories take concepts and make them understandable. They also communicate vision and hope. Jesus led by communicating well with those he wanted to follow him.

Leaders in the Church should follow Jesus' example. Every experience should be part of a grand overall strategy to lead change. Every communication opportunity should be grasped and used for leading change. Even though a leader may be communicating with an individual, the leader needs to be thinking of how the words being spoken will impact the body as a whole entity. Also, like Jesus, leaders need to become experts at telling stories and using them appropriately to lead change. Remember that God's preferred communication technique in the Scriptures is narrative.

An Overview

The next chapter focuses on a positive appreciation of leadership. The dearth of leaders is most noticeable in the Christian Church. We do not emphasize leadership in our identities, and we have downplayed the need for it; in some cases we have spoken strongly against it. The ineffectiveness of most congregations and denominations has led to a theology of smallness that validates our sickly existence and makes us feel better about it. Discussing success, effectiveness, and bold visions in such an environment is frowned upon. It is written off as too much interest in numbers, pride, or ego and as making something fleshly out of that which is spiritual. This attitude, coupled with the infamous stories of pastoral dictators (most of whom did not finish their spiritual pilgrimage well), asserts that leadership, if not sinful, is at least dangerous and that most people should avoid it. The next chapter addresses leadership not in terms of characteristics or personalities but in terms of that which produces God-ordained missions and helps to achieve awesome visions.

Chapter 3 describes the "change strategy" and what leaders need to do to communicate that strategy well to followers. Leaders now know that leading dysfunctional congregations to health demands specific, strategic choices. Leaders also know that helping effective organizations move to greater effectiveness demands that the change strategy be followed. The goal in this chapter and those that follow is to provide specific tactics that might be implemented as the strategy is being carried out. It describes the key positive images that must be communicated if a group is to be open to change.

Key Positive Key negative images.

With the communication of key positive images, there must also be the equally apparent communication of key negative images. Chapter 4 shows how the positive and negative work together. It also offers specific tactics leaders in congregations can employ to communicate both the negative and the positive in a positive manner.

While leaders are communicating in a positive manner, they are also gathering followers who will be instrumental in helping them achieve change. As in any group endeavor, different people play different roles. Some will help actually lead the charge for change. Others will be significant workers who implement the change. Key people will be mobilized to intercede with Jesus to help the right changes take place and to remove behaviors that detract from the Church's mission. No change is worth leading, especially with the pain that will be experienced, if it does not ultimately please Jesus.

While leaders are communicating the right messages and gathering specific disciples for key tasks, they are also preparing for the time when the change will actually happen. (The change process is not a sequential recipe to be followed step-by-step but rather is a multifaceted strategy by which numerous tactics are employed simultaneously). Good leaders not only anticipate the future, but they also understand the hard path that must be followed to achieve the anticipated future. The cost will be paid not only by the leaders but also by their spouses and, sadly, sometimes their children. Highly dysfunctional congregations become that way over time. Leading such congregations to change takes time, and costs emotionally. In many cases, a leader may spend three to five years communicating and implementing a change strategy before the actual change occurs. Good leaders use that time to prepare wisely for the eventual removal of barriers and the creation of incentives that produce systemic change rather than incremental change.

After laboring hard to employ change tactics as part of an overall strategy, leaders may need the help of a good interventionist to clear the final hurdles that make systemic change a reality. A few pastors are gifted enough in leadership to do this within their own personal resources. However, most pastors, like business people in the corporate world, may at some point in time need someone from the outside who functions as both a prophet and a facilitator for change. Such interventionists can slingshot the process and move the organization to higher levels of effectiveness, particularly if they are building on the work of a good leader who has been preparing people well for the needed change. Chapter 7 covers who should do such interventions, how they should be done, and the proper timing for such events.

Once systemic change begins, leaders must move quickly to embed new DNA into the congregation. This means that leaders must already have in place a plan that takes full advantage of the congregation's openness to change at a given point in time. The plan will be refined as it is implemented over time. However, when systemic change is occurring, there is no time to invent the wheel. It is time to put the new wheel on the axle and take the cart into a whole new direction. Chapter 8 discusses not only how leaders communicate this plan but also how they communicate to ensure its acceptance and embrace by the congregation.

Our culture is changing rapidly, and if we do not change, we will lose the ability to effectively influence it for Jesus. God calls for new paradigms. This is true throughout the Bible and the history of the Church. While it is true that the gospel of Jesus Christ is an unchanging message, given to us by an immutable God, we are partners with Jesus in bringing about the kingdom of God. The way we encounter the world with this message has constantly changed for over two thousand years and continues to change at an even greater pace in the twenty-first century.

My job.

Your purpose as a church leader is to lead a congregation to find those strategies and tactics that will enable followers to effectively reach lost and dying people with the good news. God calls you to lead change not only with individuals but also with groups of people, called congregations. When you take on that direct task, the ministry of the gospel is filled with vitality, risk, and excitement. Therefore, communicate well to lead well—to become a good steward over the followers that God has entrusted to you.

CHAPTER TWO
Will All the Real Leaders Please Stand Up?

In the year 2000, four leaders from a national denomination in another wealthy nation visited the American Baptist Churches of the West. For eight days, they traveled hundreds of miles, meeting each day with groups of pastors. During the meetings, these leaders simply interviewed pastors about themselves, their ministries, how they were leading congregational transformation, and how the region was helping them accomplish the difficult task of leading change.

In one case, these leaders had dinner with two lay leaders who God was using to lead change in a congregation without a pastor. The denominational leaders were amazed that systemic, transformational change could occur with the region teaming up with two key lay leaders in a small, family-oriented congregation in a small town. Such change eventually required these lay leaders to confront relatives who almost viewed the church as belonging to them because they had been there forever and had built the buildings.

At the end of the eight days, these leaders were asked to provide feedback on what they had seen and experienced. There were two major responses. The first was that these leaders, all of whom had at one time been pastors, had never seen pastors cooperate with each other so well. Their experience was that most pastors compete with each other. But their experience when interviewing the ABCW pastors was just the opposite. The second response was that the pastors they met were, for the most part, ordinary pastors. There were two or three who were obviously star leaders. But most were like pastors who were a part of their own denomination—women and men called from all walks of life with a wide variety of gifts, talents, and personalities. Overall they were quite ordinary! We often hear similar comments from leaders who visit the region that is now called Growing Healthy Churches. Most of the pastors are average people who are willing to take on the behavior of leaders because that is what God is calling them to do.

The final note to this story is that upon returning home all four of these denominational leaders resigned. They said that they have not done the job of leading and should therefore turn over the responsibility to others. It is perhaps one of the greatest acts of spirituality ever demonstrated by people in such positions. Their action allowed that denomination to make some major systemic changes and see congregations again begin to grow.

Behavior not Giftedness.

Leadership Behavior Is a Practice, Not a Gift

The Church, like the rest of the world, faces a dearth of leadership. Not only are pastors and others in churches often unwilling to assume the role of leadership (perhaps by denying the role for themselves), but also they sometimes speak against and treat leaders with great suspicion, complaining about issues of power and authority. In effect, we have now developed a theology of smallness that validates the ministries of most congregations that are both few in number and ineffective in achieving consistent fruitfulness. This is especially the case when fruitfulness is measured by the miniscule number of new disciples entering God's kingdom through the ministries of most congregations.

Another issue that always arises when discussing leadership is the nature of the qualities or characteristics that make someone a leader. We have been told in the past that leadership is related to one's talents or abilities, one's personality, or even one's situation. Those who are natural leaders—or in spiritual terms, those who have the gift of leadership—seem to validate these perceptions. However, we now know that many people have been effective leaders while seeming to defy all the formal descriptive categories of leadership. Also, many people have been placed into positions of leadership in which they have achieved greatness even though they seem to lack those talents and personality characteristics that are deemed essential for leading.

In light of the current Christian cultural context, which often de-emphasizes leadership, let's think about leadership in terms of tasks

Leadership Tasks and practices.

and practices. First, according to Leith Anderson, leadership involves a person seeing a need and taking the responsibility to see that the need is met. In this view, leadership is defined by the task of leading and not by the type of person who is taking on the responsibility. This perspective implies that if someone who has taken responsibility for meeting a need that has yet to be met, then he or she must exercise influence to mobilize followers to assist in meeting the need.

Second, leadership refers to the employment of disciplines that people can develop regardless of their talents or mix of spiritual gifts. Each personality will employ these disciplines with mixed results, but one who learns these disciplines well can find satisfactory help when leading. From time to time, God has called forth a few persons who are either naturally or supernaturally gifted for leadership. However, many believers may be called upon at specific times to exercise influence over followers who need to be mobilized to accomplish a task. Also, believers may take on leadership tasks that require them to act like leaders whether they want the title or not. This is often the case for pastors who are called upon to lead congregations in transformational change, whether gifted to do so or not. Such people can at least work at the disciplines of leadership with a level of self-awareness to know when they need help to complete the task.

Passion

At the heart of all effective leadership is passion. Although not all passionate people are leaders, one must have passion to be a good leader. That said, passion can be directed incorrectly. Many effective but morally bankrupt leaders are passionate about their goals and agendas, which are selfish and, in some cases, destructive. Other leaders have been passionate about achieving immoral missions and evil visions. However, notwithstanding the goal or the end, one will not be an effective leader without passion.

In the spiritual world, passion comes from God's work in our lives. It begins with a sense of prophetic burden that God's Spirit places

If I Lack passion, is it because I don't see God working in my life?

in our innermost being. Passion arises when we are focused on God and are able to see the needs that people have because of the great chasm between them and God. God then impresses upon us the desire to address human needs by mobilizing other children of God to build bridges that span the chasm. When this occurs, we realize that God has put in our innermost being a fire that cannot be quenched until the God-given task is fulfilled. Usually passion starts with our brokenness before a holy God that in turn generates a fire with an unrelenting sense of responsibility to fulfill the task God has called us to complete.

We live in a time when many say they are called by a God who seems to have forgotten to equip them for the task at hand. One cogent observer suggests that the present-day concept of a *call to ministry* may be related more to a dysfunctional pathology than to a well-lived spirituality. Not only is there a lack of apparent gifting but also a lack of passion. Too few persons in leadership positions have a righteous indignation that motivates them to lead well in order to address major spiritual needs. Often pastors, staff members, and lay leaders are willing to honor and acquiesce to those dysfunctional leaders who control outcomes through loud clamoring and passive-aggressive behaviors. Meanwhile, lost people are dying because the congregations in their midst will not confront such sin. We can tell if people are truly called by whether they possess a passion for God and for reaching the lost. Those who are called are willing to risk their career for the things that last.

The good news is that passion can be developed. It is not derived from our personalities or pathologies. Even someone as fearful and powerless as Esther (a woman in a male-dominated society) acted with courage and disregard for her life because she cared passionately for her people. Passion comes as we, in our own ways, take God seriously. It means seeing God as Isaiah did, knowing God as Moses did, and seeing the world as Habakkuk did. Throughout Scripture, individuals not only acted out of passion but also completed tough tasks because they were passionate about their relationship with God. Abram left all because he believed God's promise about the land and his descendants. Moses stood before

Pharaoh despite his inability to speak. Joshua and Caleb said, "Let's take the land." Gideon became a committed coward because God convinced him to do so. Habakkuk pronounced a judgment against himself and his nation because God said, "Trust me." Mary had what many neighbors believed to be an illegitimate child because she did what God called her to do.

Jesus Christ modeled passion when he set his face like a flint for Jerusalem, knowing that this trip would be the one where he would die for the sins of the world. His commitment to the human race and its need, coupled with his concern for doing his Father's will, sent him to the cross. Jesus was well aware that in death he was doing what was best for everyone but himself.

#1 Be clear about The mission.

A leader's first task is to be clear about the mission. A leader must then ask if this mission is one that God wants him or her to lead and if it is worth dying for (in American Christianity, "dying for" means being willing to lose one's job). If the mission honors a righteous God and meets needs that human beings face, then a leader has something about which to be passionate. This passion will motivate the leader to mobilize people to be involved in and accomplish a mission that honors and glorifies God.

#2, 3 just worth dying for?

church:
Primary customers:
= Lost People
Secondary customers:
= disciples

Congregations have two types of customers. Primary customers are the ones who are not yet part of the congregation because they do not have a personal relationship with Jesus Christ. Secondary customers are the disciples who are already involved in the congregation. These secondary customers are developed to reproduce more primary customers. When that order is reversed, or if a congregation loses sight of its primary customers, a leader will passionately do everything possible to right that situation—even if it costs friends and relationships. A leader is passionate about what to do, with whom to work, and how to expend limited resources.

Courage

The control of established congregations by people who do not want to grow and are unwilling to give up the privileges of membership is the biggest problem faced by those desiring to lead congregational change. The movement from an inward focus to an outward focus, with rare exception, demands a major shift in who controls the behaviors of the organization. Tackling this major issue demands courageous leaders who are willing to risk all for the sake of the Great Commission.

Pastors often lead change in organizations controlled by people who want to maintain the status quo and ensure that their own needs and expectations are met—at the expense of not ministering to lost people. Frequently, pastors who lead change must be willing to put their jobs, families, reputations, and pensions on the line. People who have lived a simple lifestyle, sacrificing time and money in order to earn a seminary degree, must then decide whether further sacrifice (both status and income) will be required if the congregation, which they are trying to lead through systemic change, turns on them. This is not an easy choice to make at any time; however, the costs are exaggerated if the pastor has a family or if the pastor, spouse, or children are living with disabilities that demand protection associated with various insurance plans or pensions. When leading a congregation of unwilling people to higher levels of effectiveness, risking security and significance demands a courage that may come only through engaging in considerable losses.

When a congregation sees necessary changes as unnecessary, lay leaders who support the changes risk losing friends and in some cases family members. Furthermore, these leaders may be marginalized or even ignored by a community of people who at one time valued them and their abilities. For such lay leaders, great courage is required.

The congregation may also face risks that come with systemic change. In today's culture, regardless of religious tradition, people vote with their feet and their pocketbook. If they like what is happening in a congregation, they attend and give. If they do not like what is happening, they stop coming, stop giving, or both. Congregations going through major changes find that there are often more people leaving than new people coming. As people leave, the budget gets tighter, and there is a sense of loss because many familiar faces have disappeared from worship services. Therefore, the congregation as a system or culture must be courageous if it is going to continue to implement the changes it believes are for the best.

As I have observed congregational change in our region of churches, I have seen pastors and their families attacked not only personally but also professionally. Many have had to sell their cars in exchange for less expensive models and do without phone service or administrative help because budgets were tight. Some have seen a large percentage of their Sunday worshipers leave. Yet these leaders have courageously stayed on task while changing the congregation's DNA, and today they are experiencing revival in their ministries. Many pastors tell me that they are now, finally, leading the kind of ministry they thought they would lead before they attended seminary. Not only are their congregations growing, but many are also filled with new disciples who are expanding ministry throughout the community. However, all of these pastors have spiritual scar tissue layering their souls. They never would have succeeded without a courage that enabled them to stand strong and face the onslaught often brought by good people who do and say wicked things.

Surrounding all these pastors are key lay leaders whose courage has cost them longtime relationships. These lay leaders stood up to their friends and said, "We must obey God's Great Commission above our personal interests in order to reach the spiritually deprived people who live around us." They had the courage to implement wise plans for both change and transition. Without their courage, many courageous pastors would not have survived the trauma of change. These lay leaders became the spiritual "Secret Service" to guard their pastors. They have had the courage to take "flaming arrows" (Eph. 6:16) for their God.

Flexibility

The world is changing rapidly each day. New generations are forming more quickly. Technology and information are expanding. We now live in an international world where what happens overseas affects our economy and culture as readily as if it occurred within our own borders. Ideas, strategies, and tactics that worked a few years ago are now discarded and considered passé. The culture of the United States is more influenced by and exerts far more influence through the exchange of information than by the creation of industrial goods.

What worked yesterday in one congregation produces little change today. What may help one congregation perform with a high level of effectiveness will often not work in another congregation. The numerous microcultures in which congregations are called to serve require individualized customization in order to be effective.

Congregations and denominations, which are entities with long-held traditions, are passing quickly from the scene because they have always found change difficult. More congregations die than are started each week in North America. Many denominations are propped up by endowments, foundations, or businesses. Some are morphing into associations where funding is more local than global.

This environment requires leaders to possess enormous flexibility. While leaders may be unchanging in their core beliefs and bedrock values, they must understand that effective congregational behaviors will vary from congregation to congregation. A congregation's mission will take on great variety as it is implemented in each microculture to which the congregation ministers. As effective ministry becomes more and more a bottom-up endeavor that reflects the calling and gifts of more and more believers, ministries will take on the personality of individuals in the body more than the pathology of the leader.

ministry becoming more bottom up endeavor

As I observe the effective congregations in our region, the change process, while following predictable patterns, occurs differently in every congregation. This is due in part to the varying personalities of both the leaders and the congregations as well the geographical, social, and cultural contexts in which the congregations exist. We have not directed any of our congregations to adopt any particular philosophy of ministry or suggested that they follow a certain recipe for change. Instead, we have challenged them to be missional and outward-focused, determining how they can best have impact on their local communities. The change process is therefore handled with great variety through a myriad of tactics, and it occurs in seemingly unique time schedules.

Obviously, a leader must be clear about the truth that is foundational to the entire ministry. The core value of love for those who are lost, or separated from God, does not change. The leader must also have a laser focus about the mission. Such clarity makes clear what the overall ministry of the congregation is and is not. However, the leader must recognize that once these things are established, she or he must be continuously changing. If leaders cannot handle such flexibility, they will find it difficult to let go of old behaviors and lead new initiatives, and long-term systemic change will probably not occur.

The focus of our particular region is church reproduction. When we started this focus several years ago, we had well-articulated ideas about the strategies and tactics that are required to conduct effective church planting. However, those strategies and tactics are continuously morphing as we learn, as the cultural landscape changes, and as each leader of a church plant teaches us about what works and does not work. Our auditors tell us that our regional, denominational organization is a challenge for them. During each annual audit, they observe continual change and evolving strategies. Unlike many organizations that auditors examine, where there are yearly routines, ours constantly demands new research to see how things can be done both differently and with integrity.

Missional

The Church of Jesus Christ was designed by its founder to bring about the kingdom of God, which means to effectively challenge the work, intention, and kingdom of the evil one. Therefore, the very nature and essence of the Church is to be involved in a passionate, missional effort of turning lost people into fully devoted followers of Jesus Christ. The Church was not designed to be an institution catering to the demanding membership requirements of disciples.

For the most part, the institutional church has spawned a large subculture where most of its ministries are designed to provide service and fulfillment to those who are already related to the Church's founder. As a result, the Church is losing its effectiveness not only to change the culture but also to meet its mandate of mission in the culture.

The command to make disciples requires an entirely different kind of leader than one called to oversee current disciples and perhaps grow congregations by reaching others who are already disciples. The most effective pastors today are missionaries at heart. These pastors see themselves as mobilizing disciples for the most exciting mission that anyone has ever been called to fulfill. They look at their congregation as sheep who need food, protection, and encouragement to go out collectively and individually to engage and overcome evil, which the Bible describes as a roaring lion. These pastors have an unceasing restlessness about them that can never be fulfilled until this spiritual engagement is finished, which for most of us will not happen in our lifetime. This quest has been continuing for thousands of years as leaders have developed future leaders to take on the cause of constantly invading the enemy's stronghold to reclaim those for whom our Leader died.

Finding leaders who are missional means looking for those who think strategically. Such leaders understand that business as usual will not work. They know the enemy is smart, constantly changing tactics to oppress people and keep them from their Savior. Strategic thinking requires the development of specific tactics that mobilize sheep to the best advantage to accomplish the mission.

Missional leaders are quite intentional about understanding not only the larger cultural issues that hinder the mission but also the microculture that surrounds their congregation. They realize that a large part of their job is determining how best to bridge the gap between their culture and the truth that resides within their congregation. They also know that cultural barriers to that truth must be removed so that seekers can either accept or reject the truth based upon its merits, not its cultural wrappings.

Missional leaders are open to accountability because they clearly understand that any successful mission must be determined by both the losses incurred and the number of new recruits brought into the kingdom of God. Each effort must be evaluated to see if it has produced the gains that honor the Church's founder and are blessed by the Holy Spirit. If the engagement has failed, the leader wants to know and understand why so that it does not happen again at the expense of precious resources.

accountability

Missional leaders know intellectually as well as intuitively that followers are motivated when leaders proclaim a clear vision, which is the answer to a great urgency that the leader has also communicated. People are willing to follow and risk greatly if they are convinced that the tasks and accompanying risks are going to accomplish something greater, bigger, and more wonderful than they could ever achieve on their own.

The Church in North America has lost its primary sense of mission. We spend far too much time and money engaging disciples in tasks and responsibilities that do not advance the mission. Each region of congregations should be looking for women and men who will step up, speak out, and mobilize groups of people to engage in the mission of the Church, which is to make more disciples for Jesus Christ. The more we focus on making disciples, the more evil we are able to overcome by setting people free. When people become new disciples of Jesus Christ, they must then be discipled to find their place in ministry, using their gifts and talents as prompted by the Holy Spirit to be engaged in the primary mission. Leaders who make this happen are not simply good leaders, they are biblical leaders.

Wisdom

The most dangerous people in the world are passionate, courageous, missional fools who demonstrate great flexibility in accomplishing their desires. Therefore, biblical leaders must also be wise. Wisdom is the ability to incorporate, assimilate, and synthesize biblical knowledge with human experience to produce spiritual behavior that is balanced, complete, and honoring to God. Good leaders understand not only their times but also how God is using people and organizations to minister effectively in such times.

Wise leaders view the world and the mission through the prism of God's Word. They realize that God has functioned as a missionary God since the fall of the human race. God's chief desire is that more people in more and more places will know God and love others. That is why God blessed Israel—so she, as a nation, could share that blessing with the rest of the world. After several hundred years of Israel vacillating between periods of rebellion and redemption, God the Father sent his only begotten Son to provide redemption and produce reconciliation between God and the people. Jesus then founded the church to reach across all human boundaries—Jew, Gentile, male, and female—to bring back all those who would come. Jesus provides his church with a vision of the future in which people from every tongue, tribe, and nation will stand before him, giving praise to their God. From the Fall in the book of Genesis to the apocalyptic restoration of the earth in the book of Revelation, God is at work as a missionary, bringing many in the human race back into a relationship with the Creator.

This awareness of global and creative reconciliation informs the job descriptions for leaders in the Church of Jesus Christ. They are missional because the God they serve is purposeful and missional.

Wise leaders guide but do not overrun sheep. They never ask more of their sheep than they are willing to do as leaders. However, they are also honest with those sheep that do not want to be missional. Such sheep are given the opportunity to participate in the core mandate (making disciples), but if they do not want to participate, they are not given voice or authority in how the mission will be accomplished.

Wise leaders know themselves. They realize they are just as egotistical as everyone else. They recognize they may be perceived as even more egotistical than others because they are willing to lead, which means getting out in front. However, because of their balanced sense of self, they let God put a chokehold on their desires. They do not accept the Christian cultural ideals for false piety that often take the very guts out of any kind of effective leadership. They understand that servant leadership means submitting gifts and talents first to Jesus and his mission and then to the needs of both disciples and those yet to be disciples.

The servant leader cannot, under the rubric of servanthood, enter into codependent relationships with either congregations or individual saints. Nor can the wise leader serve the carnal expectations of congregations not engaged in the Great Commission. Wise leaders know what it takes to lead a congregation to health, growth, and reproduction. The understanding of what a healthy congregation is and what it takes to produce one is clear. Just as clear is the understanding of what produces dysfunction within a congregation. Wise leaders stop dysfunction before it happens.

Positive

Leaders are positive they are going to win the engagement. They are therefore positive about their Lord's ability to go before them and produce victory. They are positive about their followers. These leaders believe that the Spirit's work of sanctification is real, and they presume therefore that most disciples want to serve their Lord, want to be engaged in effective ministry, and are willing to sacrifice their time and dollars when what they are doing is showing significant spiritual return for what has been invested.

Positive leaders are constantly showing disciples what God can do and wants to do, and how God is delighted to use disciples to bring about the kingdom of God. These leaders do not lead by compulsion, using guilt to get people to serve. Rather they cast vision, assume the best, and then develop new leaders and disciples who have been convinced that they can do many things in time and space that will have eternal value.

These leaders are positive because they understand that success is determined by the implementation of strategies that result in a fulfilled vision. On the night before he was crucified, Jesus told his disciples that he had accomplished the task his Father had sent him to do. He saw his ministry as successful, even though he did not travel to every corner of the globe. God has not called anyone to reach the whole world, but God calls each of us to reach the part of the world for which we have stewardship.

Biblical leaders recognize that they work for the One who will ultimately win, because God will win. Through salvation, we have been called to the winning team, led by a coach who instructs us in how to win. Christians who attempt to motivate by guilt eventually fail. Such motivation does not work because God has wired humans not to respond to service on the basis of guilt. We respond when we get a vision of a great God who has called us to great and positive things. Guilt has its place in exposing sin, keeping us humble, and remaining dependent upon God, but vision and excitement are what motivate others for service.

Responsibility

Leaders do not blame others if the mission fails. Leaders realize that good leadership means each person must take responsibility for what occurs, either positive or negative. Church leaders often avoid accountability like a plague because the review process determines who is responsible for either success or failure.

Every place I go in the world, I hear excuses about why a congregation, denomination, or ministry cannot grow. The most frequent type of excuse is an environmental one. "Our congregation cannot grow because we are in an urban, rural, or suburban location." "We cannot grow because we are in a vacation or resort area, or we are near a military base where people are constantly transferred, or the population around in is growing, declining, or static." Or, "The average age of our congregation is over sixty." No matter what the environment, there are excuses. Yet in each of these environments, people can name the two or three congregations that are growing.

The second category of excuse is a lack of commitment. Some leaders say (or think), "If my people [my board, our congregation, or our denomination] were just more committed, we would see more service, have more dollars, and see growth." Again, note that other congregations are growing because they set high expectations even in the midst of those making excuses about competition with the media, lethargy of bureaucracy, and lack of grants.

The last category of excuse is the spiritual one. "God has left this county," or "God is judging this town or city, and therefore we cannot grow."

The first excuse is really a missionary issue. The leader has not cracked open the local culture to find the keys that will help people first to hear the truth and then be open to it. The second excuse is a vision problem. A lack of commitment means a lack of vision. The last excuse is one of denial, saying that God has written off the people in a particular location. These three excuses are leadership issues. Good leaders know how to penetrate the culture, can cast vision, and are willing to believe that God wants the Church to win, replacing the evil empire with the kingdom of God. Strong leaders know what they do not know, so they get the information or the training they need. Good leaders take responsibility and will not accept excuses to get them off the hook.

As we look for leaders for congregations in our region, this list of leadership behaviors represents the key indicators of an effective future missionary. When interviewing, or rather pursuing, a potential candidate, we are not looking for specific personalities or gifts. A congregation is desperate for leaders who are filled with passion, have already demonstrated courage, see flexibility as a virtue, are missional because of their passion, are wise, really believe God expects them to win with a whole groups of saints who feel the same, and who take bottom-line responsibility for what God will do through them.

Passion
Courage
Flexibility
Missional
Wisdom
Positive
Responsibility

CHAPTER THREE
I See a Better Tomorrow

As Pastor Wilkens sits in the study that first Sunday morning, her mind wanders from sermon rehearsal to the next few years. The bishop had wanted her in this particular parish, and the congregation was greatly in favor of her coming. The previous four pastors had been disasters, and the three before them had practiced the first plank in the Hippocratic Oath: they did no harm. Right now the expectations are so high, but the prospects are so dismal. Attendance and participation has been going down for at least fifteen years. Older people can reminisce about the glory days when worship attendance was three times the current size, young people were excited, and the community recognized the congregation as influential. Today, however, survival is the current vision, and stabilizing declining numbers and dollars could be the biggest achievement. The congregation, like the downtown community in which it exists, is irrelevant to the majority of the citizens. Pastor Wilkens wonders what difference her tenure, probably a short one, will mean for her and the congregation. Can she make a difference, or is it her role to maintain and keep the ship from sinking?

Someone Has a Vision

Vision does not necessarily start with the pastor. However, most pastors who arrive to lead congregations that lack vision, hope, and morale will find that if they do not generate vision, no one else will. Committees, vision communities, or people exploring vision as a short-term project do not generate visions that produce systemic change. Vision is derived from the passion of a leader who has a prophetic fire burning within the soul to accomplish something significant for God. Groups may take this vision, help produce congregational ownership, and delineate its implementation, but, without prophetic fire to begin with, there are no images of preferred futures that produce systemic change. If pastors are not clear

images

about either their role or that of the Church, most congregations will remain dormant, irrelevant to life change, and in decline.

It is true that good saints in each congregation may see the congregation's mission as described earlier. Obviously, pastors will need to partner with such people and enlist them in the quest. However, with the nature of congregations in wealthy nations today, regardless of denominational loyalty, if the pastor does not see this mission and is not willing to assume the role of leader, systemic change will not occur. Yet even if a pastor does see the mission and undertake the leadership role, there is no guarantee that systemic change will occur. The reason is that the biblical mission of the Church is 180 degrees opposite to the mission or purpose of most congregations in such countries. *ou ch!*

Developing the Vision

A pastor who starts a new ministry in a typical, dysfunctional congregation that is either on a plateau or in decline must realize that many (or all) of the congregants do not understand the congregation's mission and the pastor's role in that mission. Therefore, the pastor must think in terms of two zones, each with particular goals and strategies.

The first zone is a period of one to five years when the leader is preparing the congregation for systemic change. This time zone is the least understood and therefore most ignored by pastors who attempt to lead change, but ignoring this zone is a major impediment to systemic change. The goal is to get the congregation ready for systemic change. The strategy employed is the focus for most of this book.

The second zone is one that works best within one year, although it may take two. If it takes longer than two years, systemic change has been thwarted and the effects will inoculate the congregation against such change for the next decade or two. The goal in this time zone is to actually lead systemic change, which means that the leaders of the congregation are those who agree with God's missional purpose for the Church and can implement it without fear of being replaced. When this condition occurs, systemic change has occurred. The congregation now has more health than sickness, it can and will grow, and it will achieve its God-given vision. Success in this time zone will only be achieved after success in the first time zone.

The initial tactic of the leader's strategy for the first zone is to pray cosmically, perceiving the congregation as a growing, powerful entity in the mind's eye. Perhaps during prayer a leader might imagine that God moves across a chessboard to bring pawns, rooks, knights, bishops, kings, and queens into the kingdom community as new disciples. Or, using another analogy, the pastor prays that God will make the congregation into a growing, healthy antibody that attacks and gobbles up spiritual infections throughout the community.

Cosmic praying also means perceiving the community in which the congregation exists as a large, complex social unit that, if targeted correctly, can be changed in large measure by servants who fight with love and grace against the evil that persists throughout the layers of our culture.

Cosmic praying is looking at the present congregation as a small unit with no influence that will become a large entity that successfully offers God's grace to an entire community, city, county, or state. Cosmic praying moves us from thinking about individuals, whom were described throughout most of chapter 2, to thinking about how God wants to consistently and regularly leverage a body of disciples to make more disciples.

The second tactic in developing the vision is to exegete the community. This begins with prayerfully walking, riding, and driving through the community—looking at the community through the eyes of Jesus Christ. It means researching everything that reflects the community's values, interests, desires, and aspirations. This research occurs through reading local newspapers, Web sites, blogs, and especially the editorials and letters to the editor or interactions of online bloggers. It entails picking up the local free editions

47

of community papers at stores that, while advertising different goods and services, also communicate the ordinary stories and issues that define the local people.

Interview people in various circumstances and venues.

The pastor interviews people, starting with those who are quite visible, such as the mayor, council people, community planners, school administrators and teachers, police and fire personnel, and doctors and nurses who deal with the public in the community hospital. The leader goes to malls and talks to those who are lounging on benches or sitting in coffee shops, or engages merchants who are open to talking about the community. The exegesis may mean going to garage sales or flea markets to see what people are selling and what they value. Throughout this cultural immersion, the pastor is not only interviewing the congregants but also neighbors and those with whom the pastor comes in contact each day.

At some point the pastor then takes this information, sorts it, and synthesizes it to articulate what the community values, its image of itself, its vision for the future, and how it views itself in relation to the communities that surround it.

While praying and studying the community, the pastor is becoming an expert on the congregation he or she is called to lead. This involves researching the history of the congregation to find those aspects of the DNA that now may not be noticeable but were at one time important fundamental elements of the congregation's belief, impacting key behaviors. The pastor is also taking objective stock of the gifts, talents, desires, dreams, aspirations, and abilities of those who currently attend. Initially, these spiritual assets may seem minimal, especially if the congregation is aging, declining, and losing momentum. However, the Spirit of God has not stopped working in the lives of people, and God is not limited by age or current attitudes that, if changed, can and will produce much.

Study of congregation old

Study of community in order to create a vision of how the church people can minister to the community.

When these tasks are completed in the first three to six months of the pastor's tenure, the pastor asks God to bring together the study of the congregation and the study of the community to create a vision of how this group of people, if led well, can develop a preferable future for itself and the community. At this point the missionary-minded pastor is asking God to give insight into how this body of believers can be mobilized to reach into the community in such a way that people will be attracted as disciples to Jesus Christ. The pastor is looking for ways to minister to community needs that will cause citizens to see the congregation as important, contributing, and worth listening to because it cares and is helping them achieve their dreams and aspirations. Obviously, the congregation has greater and more eternal hopes for the community, but it must start by gaining visibility and respect to have a platform from which to communicate its life-changing message.

Developing a Communication Strategy for the Vision

The pastor now creates a preaching calendar for the vision, initiating an intentional plan that determines how she or he will communicate the vision in sermons over the next one to five years. Again, this is part of preparing the congregation for systemic change. The pastor determines which sermons will focus almost entirely on vision and which sermons will contain subtle pieces of the vision through themes, narratives, and applications.

The pastor now realizes that somewhere in each sermon the "so what" question must be asked cosmically. In other words, "What does this text say to or demand as response from the congregation as a unit in relation to the particular mission that God intends to implement in the community?" The pastor needs to help the congregation see that God has not only called them as individuals to live changed lives on their own but is calling them as a Church to live a changed life as a group.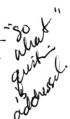

The pastor also weaves into every sermon stories of how individual disciples inside and outside of the congregation, and inside and outside of congregations elsewhere, are successfully accomplishing the mission of changing a community through the consistent and regular making of new disciples. Vision is cast primarily through well told stories with compelling metaphors.

[handwritten margin note: Talk vision at Every opportunity]

The pastor also creates a meeting calendar for communicating vision. The pastor thinks through how each worship service, board or council meeting, committee meeting, or any other meeting can be used to discuss and talk about vision, even if only for a few moments or in a few words. Worship services in which the pastor is preaching on vision may not have any other elements regarding vision in them, since the entire sermon is on that subject. However, when sermons are not wholly related to this core vision, one can communicate the vision in the announcements, when the offering is taken, through the call to worship, or at some other point in the service.

[handwritten margin note: Pastor speaks to vision at all board meeting]

Most pastors have a designated time to speak during the board or council meetings. Some of this time in every meeting should be used to discuss vision. Sometimes it may simply be a story about someone in the congregation who has behaved in such a way that a parable of the vision is demonstrated.

It is important to understand that every phone call, e-mail, conversation, and interaction with someone in the congregation can be a crucial moment for casting vision. There are no throw away conversations while the pastor is on duty. And when it comes to communicating vision, it is a 24/7 task; the pastor is never off duty. The people will learn that whenever they interact with the pastor, the conversation will always be steered toward how God is calling this congregation to see a steady stream of new disciples who are following Jesus Christ. Preferably, the congregation will know the good qualities (see chapter 2) that are part of the pastor's character. However, the people should also know that the pastor possesses a tenacious spirit in communicating a vision that God is designing for this particular congregation.

[handwritten margin note: See congregation as the place God is always at work]

The pastor needs to believe that God's Spirit is at work in the lives of congregational members. This means the pastor is always seeing the congregation in its best light, hoping for the best, and telling stories of those who are doing things well. Individual and congregational confrontations will come when systemic change is attempted. However, vision never takes root in people when it is communicated through guilt, or acts of warfare. Vision is always cast in a positive light.

The pastor is also looking for those within the congregation who are responding to the sermons, training, and comments on vision. Their responses may range from resounding compliments about the ideas to sarcastic statements putting down those who seem to have no vision. In any case, such people are at least open to God's preferable future for the congregation. The pastor may enlist some of these individuals to help with the community or congregational research mentioned earlier. The pastor works at feeding their imaginations while encouraging them to share their thoughts and dreams with others.

Finally, while the pastor is sewing the seeds of vision, the pastor is fulfilling well those ministries and responsibilities that are designed to keep the congregation small and effective at meeting member needs. Failure to do so will cause the pastor to lose credibility and reduce any future leverage for change. The pastor still functions as a chaplain: visiting, caring, and counseling. The pastor still attends the endless committee meetings that produce no growth and re-enforce the power of the church bosses. The pastor fulfills all the expected roles required in highly dysfunctional congregations, realizing they are providing future political capital to lead change.

keep at the things expected but not as impactful.

At this time the pastor is really living a double life, or at least performing two jobs, a chaplain and a leader. This is one major reason why change is so difficult and why most pastors decide, often unintentionally, not to pursue it. The job is just too demanding. It is much easier to go with the flow. Going along well creates job security, demands few if any risks, and is ultimately not too tough of a workload. In fact, in many cases it can be quite comfortable, though many pastors are like some farmers who always talk as though the sky is falling tomorrow.

Dying congregations, whose only vision is that the congregation remain viable enough for long-term members to have their funerals in the church building, often have no one left who can dream. Many may be able to reflect on the glory days of the past, while few if any can still dream dreams of God's abundant blessing on their congregation. In such cases, even the idea of a vision usually must start with a person new to that setting. In most cases the new person is the new pastor. This is in some ways good because it allows the pastor to paint on a blank canvas, at least in relation to the vision. If the pastor has no vision, does not think in visionary leadership terms, and will not work at developing a vision, then his or her tenure is doomed to maintenance at best and the hastening death of the congregation at worst.

On the bottom line of change, everything is reduced to leadership. The best and only thing a leader can do in a desperate situation is to go back to vision. If no one else in a congregation can dream, then the pastor must act like a leader and focus on vision. Without vision there is no hope.

CHAPTER FOUR
When Is Somebody Going to Do Something?

As Everett drives home, his wife talking on her cell phone, he reflects on the pictures that have been coming to mind with greater regularity. He has lived in this community for most of his life and has enjoyed the comfort that comes with the familiar avenues, stores, and surroundings that make up his hometown. But he knows that just below the civility of raking leaves in the fall, caroling at Christmas, perusing garage sales in the spring, and watching Little League in summer, there are major problems. Most people, including members of the congregation he attends, ignore church, seeing it as irrelevant to their lives. Behind many of the painted doors and manicured lawns, families are disintegrating. Divorce, separations, affairs, and spousal abuse are the norm more than the exception. The junior and senior high schools are different from when he attended. Drug use is common among many of the students, and their parents' use of drugs and alcohol are setting the example. People can count on Everett's community to give to disaster relief but not to care for the poor and immigrant groups doing the work no else in the county wants to do. The saddest part is that despite all the rhetoric in his church, little is ever done. And the limited financial and human resources in the aging and dying congregation circumscribes what the congregation tries to do. Everett believes that Jesus—the Jesus he follows —wants people to give him their allegiance and that such allegiance should mean both individual and corporate vitality. But Sunday after Sunday, Everett leaves worship feeling a lack of hope for himself, his congregation, and the community he dearly loves.

Good Vision Is Rooted in Urgency

Faith, love, and hope are crucial motivations for a life in Christ, according to Paul's letter to the Corinthians (1 Cor. 13). Paul asserts that in human relationships, love takes priority over faith and hope. But when it comes to knowing God and having a relationship with Jesus Christ, faith takes priority over love and hope. Finally, when it comes to survival and to living with spiritual zest, hope takes priority over faith and love. Although people can survive without feeling love or exercising faith, without hope they become severely depressed and may even take their own life. That is why vision is crucial both for individuals and for groups of people, whether small congregations or large nations. Vision is God's major tool to provide hope for people. Vision is God's way of helping people see a preferable future that can bring meaning, fulfillment, and wholeness to their existence.

If such is the case, why do so many hopeless congregations in North America not respond to vision? The answer is that when people are presented with a choice between maintaining the status quo and moving toward new vision, they almost always reject the new vision. New visions require risk, which entails leaving that which is known and comfortable for that which is unknown. People are afraid that the unknown may turn out worse than what they are currently experiencing. Fearing risk and the unknowns that accompany change, most people opt for what is present and known. And they do so even if such an experience means living in highly dysfunctional environments, lacking meaningful engagement with life, and eventually dying. The assumption is: "The worst [death] will not occur while I am here."

Good leaders understand that the presentation of vision must always, always be accompanied with a presentation of urgency for that vision. Without the consistent presentation of urgency, people vote with their behavior for the status quo. A good leader makes the status quo so unacceptable that people are willing to embrace a new vision. Congregations that perceive they have the necessary financial and human resources to survive are often the hardest to lead to change. The status quo for the congregation may not be great or even good, but many believe it to be better than what a risky, unknown change might produce. And until someone can convince them that the status quo is unacceptable, people will not change, no matter how compelling the new vision might be.

For example, preschools are key ministries that serve viable felt needs in the community and often provide congregations with a consistent income that allows them to conduct ministries they might not otherwise be able to pursue. However, in our region, preschools often become living endowments that allow congregations that are dying or even dead to operate. Without these preschools, some congregations would cease to exist. But the steady income allows a handful of people in a highly dysfunctional congregation to avoid change or deny death.

Therefore, good leaders must spend as much time creating urgency as they do communicating a new vision, thereby making the congregation uncomfortable with the status quo. Wise leaders always give people a choice between a preferable future and an unacceptable present.

Developing Congregational Urgency

Urgency must first be created, at least in the mind and heart of the leader, through a theological perspective. Other urgencies for change may be valid in that they meet real human and cultural needs, but if there is no theological or biblical basis for the urgency, then the congregation might as well cease to exist. Social and cultural needs can and often are met by organizations that start when someone has a passion to meet a particular need. Such agencies are valid and deserve our support. However, the Church of Jesus Christ was designed to do much more than meet the social needs of individuals and cultures. Jesus said he was establishing his Church to defeat the "Gates of Hell" (Matt. 16:18). Ultimately, the Church was designed to meet a spiritual need. Attention to the spiritual need results in the motivation to deal with social and cultural needs.

The most basic question for any Christian is whether a person living in this world is a lost individual, spiritually separated from God and at risk of eternal separation from the source of all mercy, love, and grace. If the Christian leader acknowledges the risk of eternal separation from God, then do lost people matter to God? And do lost persons matter enough that God wants them to hear a message of good news that Jesus died and rose again to remove the sin that separates them from God? Can the Christian leader articulate this good news or gospel in such a way that a lost individual believes in that message and is reconciled to God to experience a new life in Christ? If this view of God, Jesus, and the gospel is the core reason for the existence of the Church, then every congregation has an urgency to get this message to as many people as possible. It is the ultimate, though not the only, reason for the existence of the Church. The mandate of the Church is to be God's instrument through which needy people learn of divine grace and appropriate that grace to one another through faith in Jesus Christ.

Perhaps the greatest sin of denominations and most congregations is the lack of urgency to bring the good news to lost individuals. Congregations usually believe an historically orthodox message. Yet they practice passive and sometimes active disdain for sharing the faith with any sense of urgency. Most congregations behave as though God is going to somehow give their neighbors a pass to escape divine judgment for their unrepentant sins, whether that consequence is eternal separation from God after death or something more severe. In other words, even churches that teach an urgent message are often unwilling to implement it.

One reason that our region has experienced a significant number of congregational transformations, plus a growing number of congregational reproductions, is that many leaders in distinct congregations decided to take this concept of urgency seriously. As we work with dying congregations, we often tell the people that their congregation is not merely dying but also disobedient. We explain how the congregation has for years believed an urgent message but lived for itself, making few if any new disciples and failing to fulfill the mission that Jesus had designed for his Church. Our first recommendation in this type of situation is a day of prayer in which clergy and lay leaders alike lead the congregation to confess the sin of complacency (no urgency).

After this confrontation, most congregations are then open to a new vision. They come to grips with the status quo, and it becomes unacceptable. These congregations are no longer content merely to live for themselves but desire to reach out with urgency to those who face the most critical need of life, a decision about their eternal destiny. $LOST NESS$

Pastors who are alone in preparing a congregation for change must first ask themselves the question of spiritual urgency. Do they really believe that the majority of the people in our communities are lost to God and that being lost matters deeply to God? They must also ask if the mission of their congregation is to join Jesus' mission for the Church, which is to make new disciples? If leaders can answer these questions in the affirmative, then they must begin to develop a strategy of communicating this urgency.

Pastors can communicate spiritual urgency as they discuss the purpose and nature of the Church and describe how that core purpose is manifest in a local congregation. Pastors can also help congregations to see those who do not know Christ in the same way that Christ viewed humanity when on earth. Jesus did not see those who were apart from him as enemies of God, nor did he view their sins as attacks on God. Instead, Jesus viewed those who were apart from him as lost sheep in need of leaders who would lead them to become his disciples through love and compassion. Pastors can also create urgency by revisiting the biblical themes about eternal issues (love, justice, judgment, mercy, atonement, and more), which today are often ignored in practice.

Urgency for a new vision, which leads to systemic change when implemented, can be generated from a number of perspectives. However, there is no need to go through these exercises if the spiritual urgency is not real. The work is too hard and the payoff is not worth the investment if the passion to share the good news is buried. Preferably, none of us is in the business of saving congregations or denominations. No organization or institution is worth the pain if the primary reasons for renewal are temporal. But if the reasons are eternal and ultimately spiritual because they are in tune with God's heart, then the gain far outweighs any pain. The whole purpose of congregational transformation is to get congregations once again fulfilling God's mission. Such urgency produces awesome visions and, in our experience, awesome results.

A second way to create urgency is to help a congregation see where it is headed if it does not change. This method is far more pragmatic but often just as effective. We have found that congregations fairly far down the life cycle are easier to lead change in than those only halfway down the life cycle. It is easier to show those close to death that the end is near. Most congregations have a greater fear of dying and ceasing to exist than of changing. Of course, many of the congregations nearing death live with terminal doses of denial and will not accept the fact they are almost dead. However, once the risk of death permeates the congregation, this fear creates an urgency that allows a vision to be born.

In our region, we have often shown congregations the year and month (with some preciseness) that they will no longer be able to pay their pastor, afford health and other kinds of insurance, and have people alert enough to take care of basic day-to-day business. In some cases, sadly, the congregation decided to cannibalize itself by selling off property, creating mixed marriages of merger with other dying congregations that only postponed the inevitable, or disguising the situation by renting facilities to other congregations. Such actions did not bring health to the congregation, only a living endowment.

The good news for many congregations is that there is a great fear of a congregation's death. People have collectively and individually invested in the life of the congregation. They know that at one time God used it mightily to minister to the community. People do not want to see this investment lost. Therefore, a good communicator with great legitimacy leverages that fear to help motivate the congregation to aspire to better things. In the process, the congregation is motivated because it has come to find the present situation unacceptable.

A third way to develop urgency is to help people see with stark reality the community in which the congregation exists. Increasing paganism within the culture produces a decline in moral standards. As these standards decline, behavior consistent with such standards also declines. Individuals make many more poor choices that contribute to a greater numbers of behaviors leading to personal disaster and frustration. The nuclear family is becoming almost as extinct as dinosaurs, resulting in many children who are raised without mothers or fathers or both. In most states, the government is the "parent" of at least ten thousand children in custody on any given day. In our culture, many children with a mom and a dad are raised as though they had neither. Media and drugs make all kinds of sinful behavior more available and easier to become secretly involved with. Economic issues continue to divide people, creating financial excuses for people to live sinfully.

Weakened congregations have neither the resources nor the stamina to take on many of the problems of those attending worship services. And they clearly have little time, money, or human resources to address the needs at a community level. Therefore, the more people can see how these needs affect human beings who live around and among them as well as how the social needs affect the congregation, the greater the sense of urgency a pastor can communicate.

These problems, described here in a general way, are found in all parts of our country and in other highly developed nations. Though these problems are seen (or hidden) differently in various neighborhoods, they are real and impact how we live. It may be more difficult in some locations (especially where the members of the congregation live in insulated or gated enclaves) to help people see and experience such needs. The job of the pastor is to ferret out the cultural problems and needs and then find ways to communicate the big picture to the people.

As with describing human needs, when describing societal needs, the pastor must project the vision with urgency. Jesus has designed his Church to minister to both individuals and communities. The leader's job is to show how a healthy, vibrant, growing congregation can again begin to make a difference in the lives of individuals as well as those within the community.

A fourth way to create urgency is to help the congregation feel the loss of the people who have left because the congregation was no longer healthy, vibrant, and growing. Many congregations that are in decline or on a long-term plateau have at least one generation missing. Sometime in the past, as the congregation began to move down the life cycle and lose its health, there was a conflict or struggle. Perhaps the pastor was incompetent, the congregation would not change the style of worship, or controlling lay leaders prevented certain people from "gaining too much power" by using their positions to make others uncomfortable. In any case, good people left the congregation. Usually, the people who left or were run off were leaders who served well and gave well. This group of people is usually never replaced in the life of the congregation. As the congregation ages, the group leaves a generational hole in its body. The congregation feels the loss of these leaders for a long time—in the loss of leadership, the loss of giving, the loss of wisdom, and the loss of passion and courage for ministry. So the pastor might point out that the congregation has no teenagers because many parents left when the children were reaching junior high age, but the leaders would not hire a youth pastor. Or, ten years later, the third pastor in six years might point out that the same generation is still missing, at an age when they would be good givers with more financial resources.

Most dysfunctional congregations do not attract healthy leaders. However, they often attract leaders who are unhealthy emotionally and spiritually. Such people, including some pastors, prey on congregations for their emotional and spiritual well-being until there is no feeding left to do. They then leave. After the predatory leaders leave, the congregation's prospects have worsened because more people have gone. So the congregation needs to feel the loss of the healthy people who have been run off by poor leadership.

Finally, one can create urgency by describing what is happening in our culture as a nation. Many church people, particularly those who are older, preserve an image that the United States is a Christian nation. This perception is not true of other wealthy nations. Christians in other regions of the world understand that they live in nations that are hostile to Christianity as an institution and as a movement. But in the U.S.A. many people, particularly in Bible Belt areas, believe we are a godly nation. Although the themes and images of Christianity still run strong throughout the nation, even in the appeal of political candidates who seek rulership, most alert observers realize that Christendom is over. The state and the culture are now more hostile to Christians. Actual church attendance and involvement is on the decline and has been for more than thirty years. Most congregations are either on a plateau or in decline. New church plants are not keeping up with congregational deaths. The morality of those who attend churches is often little different from those who do not attend and who profess not to be Christians. And finally, most congregations have little or no impact on the communities in which they exist.

Pastors and lay leaders should find it relatively easy to gather the specific data required to show people that our nation is no longer a churched nation and that most people have no understanding of the gospel message, who Jesus Christ is, and what he expects of them in relation to his death and resurrection.

Creating Healthy Urgency

In one sense, creating urgency for a congregation is a relatively easy task. The problems for most congregations are so evident and the needs are so great that causing people to see and feel what is or is not occurring is simple. This is particularly true when one comes at urgency first from a theological perspective and then adds to that the issues related to the congregation, the community, generations, and the nation. Each of these problems relates to one another. Describing urgency is not a challenge.

If one creates urgency from a prophetic perspective so that everyone feels guilty about all that could be happening but is not, there will be no change. Prophets create guilt, and guilt is designed to produce repentance, which is a type of change. But changes in congregations, which may start with repentance, must be led by leaders rather than prophets. Shame and blame do produce change. We have all seen pastors and speakers who do well at making us feel guilty about everything we are not doing, or who work too effectively with our internal pain. While these pastors and speakers have their place in God's economy, they seldom lead change. They often create a cycle of guilt and repentance. While we need prophets, we need leaders even more.

Leaders understand that creating urgency is a tool to produce change. This tool must always be used with its companion: casting vision. People do not embrace vision without a sense of urgency, unless the status quo is so bad that it is totally unacceptable. Moses, for example, did not need to convince the leaders of Israel that living in a land of milk and honey was better than being slaves, making bricks, and having their male children killed. Moses spent little, if any, time on urgency because the danger was obvious. However, most dysfunctional congregations believe that the same old routine each week with a handful of people is nowhere close to slavery; they believe it to be closer to heaven.

Pastors must cast this type of urgency more in a descriptive manner than a prophetic one. At some point, there could be repentance. Repentance is crucial, and the Holy Spirit's leading will probably not work without it. But a congregation plunged constantly into feelings of guilt will never change. Congregations must come to believe on their own (with the Spirit's help) that their status quo is harmful and unacceptable. When that occurs, they are then ready for the hope that comes with vision.

Strategies and Tactics for Communicating Urgency

After a pastor creates a vision calendar, it should be updated with an urgency calendar. Each weekend worship service must communicate urgency (as well as vision) intentionally and by design. For example, during announcements the pastor can remind the people to bring money or groceries for the community food bank next Sunday. The pastor might then refer to records or memories from years ago when the congregation was the leading community provider for the food bank. The pastor would then commend the congregation for this wonderful heritage, even though such is not the case now. Later in the sermon, when speaking of outreach and growth, the pastor can state how one day in the future this congregation might be healthy enough to be the largest contributor of food and money to the food bank as well as to conduct other great acts of kindness and compassion. The announcement would help create urgency that prepares the way for the statement of vision in the sermon. This method of communication is positive and does not intentionally raise guilt.

A second major strategy is the further development of an urgency preaching calendar that dovetails with the vision preaching calendar. Preaching is the major way to frequently bring before an unhealthy congregation the needs that it is not addressing, while at the same time offer hope for how these needs can be met. Hope is the substance of the vision. Urgency in preaching may demand creativity for pastors who choose to preach from the lectionary each week. However, what the preacher has intentionally planned to say may be covered in the application of the text. There are also times of the year, such as Christmas, when people may be more open to hearing about urgency. These are good times to emphasize the matter.

For example, if the primary mission of the congregation is to make disciples, then the leader must consistently visit themes that talk about why it is important to be a disciple of Jesus Christ. There is the need to be reconciled to God in order to enter into a family relationship with Jesus. There is the need for forgiveness and justification. A pastor can express urgency by describing the plight of individuals who have not experienced these works of God in their lives. Vision comes as we offer God's answer to the plight of humans through the work of Jesus Christ. Therefore, congregations need to hear both the plight of those outside of Jesus Christ and his church and the offer of hope that can be accomplished as the congregation once again engages in God's mission for the Church.

Remember that as people encounter Jesus Christ, they are called to live so that both individuals and communities are changed. For congregations to have an impact upon their communities, they must be growing. As the congregation grows and gains more human resources, it has more to share with the community. One of the larger congregations in our region raised 65,000 pounds of foodstuffs in four weeks to help feed the poor in their community. They were able to have this impact because they have over fifteen hundred people in their average worship services. This example is not to diminish appreciation for what smaller congregations can do but to point out that as congregations grow they have more resources to minister with the love of Jesus Christ to their communities.

Another tactic for communicating urgency, particularly when it comes to the decline of the congregation, is to use charts or graphs. Often these tools provide quick visuals of what has been happening in worship attendance or giving over the last decade or more. Pictures may show how the worship center was full or how Sunday school had more than one hundred children only five years ago. Sometimes putting pictures of the past next to pictures of the present may say more than any words could ever say. Pictures might also remind the congregation of the leaders and servants who left because they were forced out.

A pastor might use each of these tactics at times of anniversary. Again, the leader can talk about the great days through which God led this congregation. Pictures of the past may be visual celebrations of God's grace. Pictures of the present may then be tied to vision, with a prayer for the room to be filled with people several times every weekend.

Another effective tactic to help communicate urgency related to community and national needs is to use interviews. In this age, it is possible to conduct interviews either live in the worship service or by DVD. The latter gives more flexibility and can be edited to fit the time available. Interview people from the community who deal with its problems (police officers, fire fighters, emergency personnel, social workers, nurses, doctors, lawyers, judges, the mayor, city and school planners, or teachers), and encourage them to tell their stories. Ask them to tell what they have seen and experienced and how this affects them and their families. Ask what kind of help they need and how your congregation and other congregations can be involved.

Often, hearing stories from the community at large will produce individual change first and congregational change eventually. In one of our congregations, a woman in her sixties shared with her new small group how she visits under the bridges in her town every Saturday night and gives away food to homeless people. Her small group is now going with her at different times, and others are joining her regularly.

DVD interviews of people who do not attend church at all and who find it boring, irrelevant, or "not for them" are a way for people to see what is happening nationally. It might be good to have someone conduct interviews at a coffee shop or some other busy place that is filled with people during the same time the worship service is taking place. Desktop video technology allows you to do the interview one weekend and show it the next.

In the next chapter, you will read about three key teams. One way to develop urgency at this point is to take these teams on prayer drives or prayer walks. Another effective way is to take people on the teams to interview community workers at their place of employment.

God mightily blessed our region of congregations from 1997 to 2001 as we went from thirty-seven growing congregations to more than one hundred and fifty. In the process, we achieved our vision of having 70 percent of our congregations growing. With that achievement, we needed a new vision. God gave us the vision to double the number of growing congregations to three hundred by starting one hundred and fifty new congregations in ten years.

For one and a half years, I worked on casting a vision for church planting. In the middle of the second year, one of our leading pastors questioned the vision and raised the issue of whether we should implement it or not. I realized then that I had not only failed to cast the vision well but had also made an even bigger mistake. I had not created urgency for the vision. I went back to the drawing board and determined how for the next year and a half I would both create urgency and cast vision. The result has been the planting of almost thirty new congregations in three years. We are on target to accomplish our vision.

Urgency and vision go together. Without urgency, people do not usually embrace vision; they prefer the status quo. Our job, therefore, is to make the status quo so unacceptable that people will desire hope, which means embracing the vision.

Urgency and vision do not automatically produce change, but they are foundational to all systemic change. If a pastor wants to prepare a congregation for systemic change, the best thing to do is to continually communicate urgency and vision in every conversation, meeting, and service—using every opportunity—for three to five years.

CHAPTER FIVE
No One Does It Alone

Every week, Anna waited until all the women left. She enjoyed much about their gatherings—catching up on family news; interacting with women who really cared for each other; and the familiar sights, sounds, smells, and comfort of their room downstairs beneath the sanctuary. But each meeting created great disequilibrium when the discussions turned to church matters. At that point, everything became dismal. They told tales, stories, and anecdotes of the glory days with great joy and delight, often accompanied by laughter. But those days had ended twenty or more years ago. Retelling them was like enjoying memories of youth by finding some childhood heirloom in the attic, knowing that those days of zest and energy would never happen again. The mental images of the past brought back fond feelings and generated reflections of worth and significance. However, that was all they now had: memories and reflections. The great days of the congregation were a thing of the past. The talk always turned back to the present. Everyone had her own special complaint. For some, it was the condition of the building; for others, it was the newer music; a few complained about the new people and their unwillingness to fit in, especially the younger women who never attended their meetings; and almost everyone had something negative to say about either the pastor or his spouse. Anna was wise enough to know that the complaints were ultimately motivated by a loss of purpose and meaning, declining numbers, a lack of influence and status in the community, and ultimately a fear of death—not only their own individual demise but that of the congregation.

So Anna waited until everyone was gone. The pastor was at lunch, and the building was completely empty. She went into the sanctuary and laid hands on every pew, every chair in the choir loft, and the walls in the now pewless balcony. As she laid her hands on each of these objects, she prayed the same prayer, "God, please once again fill these pews, these chairs, and this area with people: children, teens, adults, families, singles, seniors, anyone." Anna had been performing this weekly ritual for eight years. As she would drive away from the church, she often wondered if she was too late or if God would one day respond to her prayers.

Leading systemic change in a dysfunctional congregation is attempting the most difficult change possible. Moving from habitual dysfunctional conduct to health, growth, and reproduction requires the change of the congregation's culture. Making such a change is analogous to one nation going to war with another. In some cases, nations attack others in order to impose their values and culture, take control of national systems, and gain economic advantage. In other cases, nations attack as a means to throw off the culture, values, and control of an imperial nation, thereby determining their own destiny and culture. In either case, there is an attempt by one nation to change the defining culture by embracing new values that will reflect a new purpose and reason for existence. Healthy, growing, reproducing congregations, which reflect a very small minority of congregations in wealthy nations, and average, normal, dysfunctional congregations, which are the majority, are two very different cultures that cannot and will not exist together. They are like two different nations with different cultures that embrace opposite values and do not usually speak the same language.

Healthy congregations are defined by sacrifice. They exist more for those who are currently not a part of the group (analogous to persons from another nation) than for those who comprise the current congregation. They are missional in their nature and, as a result, outwardly focused in orientation. They organize themselves to accomplish mission and are willing to change any organizational structure that inhibits the accomplishment of that mission.

Dysfunctional congregations, on the other hand, despite all their rhetoric about sacrifice exist more for those who already rule the congregation than for those who are on the outside. (This is not to say that such congregations do not perform many good and sacrificial behaviors but that such behaviors are never practiced in such a way that they put the congregation's existence at risk.) Such congregations are far more institutional than missional and are by nature inwardly focused. These congregations are organized to conserve the status quo and only make peripheral changes to try and adapt to new environments, usually with great ineffectiveness.

Most pastors attempting to lead systemic change do not understand the severity of the problem and the intensity of the conflict that will be produced when these two cultures begin to collide. When recruiting pastors, congregational leaders and search committees often generate statements declaring that their church seeks a new pastor to lead change. Many, if not most, pastors believe such press releases. Often, the clippings that indicate a desire for growth and perhaps even reproduction are created by well-intentioned zealots who are clueless about how the real matriarchal and patriarchal networks in most congregations function. Others who may champion such causes want change and growth as long as the well-established system that has been in place for years does not change. Most pastoral tenures are short because new pastors quickly become old pastors when they realize that the recruitment rhetoric that appointed or lured them to the congregation was not much more than propaganda.

When pastors come to most established congregations and desire to lead change, they must realize that they are signing up to lead not just a few battles but an all-out war. Most pastors fail in this war because their army is too small when the conflict is engaged. They have too few officers. They are usually outsmarted by better generals who are fighting on their home turf. They lack the required understanding and information to assess the strengths and weaknesses of the enemy. Their battle plan is flawed from the start. They often have inadequate resources (including those described in chapter 2).

This chapter offers help to pastors who are preparing to lead their congregation to a new and better culture. It will help pastors recruit the right leaders, develop a better strategy than most, and understand that the battle should never start until there are enough allies to provide a possible chance of winning. No engagement this serious will ever be won without significant spiritual resources that will foreshadow defeat if not marshaled well.

Analyzing the Situation

Each congregation has both a formal and an informal structure. The formal structure is determined by a denominational manual (e.g., A Book of Church Order, or Book of Discipline) or a set of bylaws. The formal structure is the legal framework that determines how the congregation makes decisions and carries out its normal business. However, because congregations are social organizations, there is always an informal structure. This structure reflects how most daily and weekly decisions are made and how business is normally carried out. In all congregations, there are times when the two structures overlap and reinforce one another. At other times, the two are incompatible and conflict with each other. When they conflict, the informal structure normally takes precedent unless a fight ensues and the congregation is forced to take note of the formal structure. In terms of structure, congregations are like any other social entity. The formal structure states how things should be done, and the informal structure determines how most things get accomplished.

Wise change agents work at quickly learning the two structures, noting how each functions separately and how they work together. These agents of change also invest time in determining the real leaders of the congregations and how those leaders interact with the two structures. While the real leaders may be a part of the formal structure, they often are not, choosing instead to use the informal structure to maintain their influence in the congregation. The real leaders know how to use both structures to their advantage in order to maintain their influence and stop any changes, no matter how badly they are needed, that threaten their leadership roles.

Therefore, pastors and lay leaders desiring to lead systemic change must first learn both structures and then determine how the congregation's actual leaders leverage those structures. If the actual leaders of the congregation really want change and are willing to use or to give up their influence to make the change happen, then you do not need to read this book. Just gather the leaders around you, and go for it! The tragedy in most congregations is that those in positions of leadership have gained significance in possessing these roles and are not only unwilling to sacrifice them for health and growth but will also fight tooth and nail to prevent change. Furthermore, change agents must not be fooled by the rhetoric of congregational leaders. Many will talk of the need for change while doing everything in their power to inhibit it. This is particularly true of those who brought in the pastor to lead the congregational change. When they realize that real change means a loss of their influence, they quickly turn and become the pastor's adversary.

Team One: Developing Resources

While the new pastor is communicating urgency and developing vision, he or she is also recruiting three key teams of people. Team One is a prayer team that will commit to pray regularly for changes that lead to health, growth, and reproduction. These people will regularly and consistently implore God to act and move through the congregation once again to make it a place of vital ministry, to have impact upon the community, and to make a multitude of new disciples. Team One may include only a few people, but size is not the issue. The issue is finding individuals whose hearts are broken over the condition of the congregation and the needs in the community, and who believe that the congregation is trying God's patience and compassion.

Upon recruiting this team, the pastor meets with them to pray and to train them in how to pray. The pastor should train team members to pray much more corporately than individually. (Others in the congregation should be praying for individual saints and their needs). This prayer team should see the congregation as a unit, a group of people that God desires to leverage for effective ministry. They will pray that the congregation embraces an outward-focused mission that puts the spiritual needs of those in the community above the needs of the congregation. They will pray for a compelling vision that will motivate and drive the congregation to great acts of ministry. They will pray that the congregation sees the urgency for such a mission and vision. The pastor and perhaps one or two key lay leaders should communicate this type of purpose each time the team meets.

The pastor communicates regularly what Team One is learning about urgency and vision in order to provide information for prayers. At times the pastors may want to take the team on prayer walks or drives through the community to help them gain vision and see urgency for their prayers. The pastor constantly communicates to this team "big picture" ideas that relate to urgency, vision, mission, change, the community, and the purpose of the congregation (making more disciples for Jesus Christ).

It would be helpful for the pastor to present a map of the community that the congregation will reach when the congregation once again becomes outwardly focused. The pastor might instruct the team to pray regularly for different features on the map. One idea is to have pictures of the various regions and the people who live in those areas. Consider using any visual that helps those praying to think outside the congregation, to focus the prayers on the community, and to seek a vision to reach that community.

Also the pastor might create lists of economic, social, political, educational, and other needs that people face within the community. The pastor then helps Team One understand the spiritual needs that are either reflected by or hidden within the needs listed. For example, small communities that have little (or corrupt) police protection may become havens for those using and selling drugs, or for rings of thieves. The drug issue has impact upon families, children, and the schools, ultimately leading the community to become of place of little hope and driving stable families down a spiral of despair. Congregations in such communities are facing deep spiritual issues that are often seen in social and economic problems. Teach people to pray for God's influence once again over such communities. Even without political or legal power, this influence can be brought to bear when a strong, healthy congregation is reaching out to people and meeting them at their point of need.

Since this team will meet over a number of years as the pastor is preparing for the conflict that will come, the training is to be done inductively, in meeting after meeting. Remember, the purpose of Team One meetings is prayer and more prayer. Training occurs through the focus of the prayer, not through workbook or programmatic training. The focus of the meetings is targeted prayer for the congregation to become once again an effective tool for disciple making in God's kingdom. Team One is the most crucial of the three teams because the pastor is storing up through this team spiritual resources for the engagement that will surely come.

Team Two: Developing Ideas

Team Two is the vision or dream team. Certain people find new ideas and ways of thinking intriguing and are energized when put with others who think as they do. Also many declining congregations have some individuals who are dissatisfied with the status quo and make quite clear how they feel. Idea people and critics should be recruited for this team. The purpose of this team is to help the pastor develop arguments for urgency and create vision in order to address the urgency. As the team meets and eventually begins to crystallize its ideas, it may help the pastor develop large strategic initiatives to articulate the urgency and implement the vision. Although this team may start with two or three, it should never grow past eight to ten people. As new people are recruited, the pastor may need to let go of those who cannot move from negative to positive thinking, by helping them to find other places to serve.

The pastor's responsibility is to communicate the visionary ideas that God has been developing. The pastor also shares with the team what has been learned about urgent community needs that the congregation might one day address when the human and financial resources are available. The team's next task is to conduct more research and think creatively about implementing possibilities in these two areas of need. The group should not focus on areas of concern within the congregation that are obvious (e.g., declining numbers and dollars) but should wrestle with the issues that are producing evidence of poor spiritual health and the reasons why they cannot be currently addressed. It would also be helpful to explore realistic ways to address or at least discuss these issues in more open forums. This is a good way to deal with congregational urgency.

The pastor should help this team focus on the needs within the community. The pastor might encourage members to meet with local police, emergency workers, the mayor or the mayor's staff, town or city planners, educators, social agencies (both public and private), radio and newspaper journalists, and others who have knowledge of the local culture. The purpose is to do fresh research into what these individuals perceive as needs that the community is facing. If the community is growing, there are specific needs attached to such growth; if it is declining, there are very different needs.

The pastor would then lead Team Two to prioritize community needs, indicating which ones a healthy congregation could address first and how that might be accomplished. This exercise should help this team to articulate how the pastor should develop strategies to communicate urgency and cast vision. The team might also create a priority list of specific issues and perhaps even collect stories that the pastor might use in communication. As the team synthesizes this information, it should communicate with Team One so that the issues, specifics, and stories inform their praying.

Again, this team will be meeting for several years, so everything need not be managed at one time. However, the work of the team should help the pastor to articulate clearly the urgency at hand. It should also help the pastor to articulate clearly the vision that God is placing before the congregation. Eventually, the team should help devise grand strategies for implementing vision. It is important for all the team members and the pastor to understand that it is not the team's responsibility to either communicate or help implement this information. The responsibility of the team is to generate ideas. Often, those who can generate ideas are not gifted in the area of executing those ideas. Many of the strategies for implementing vision may not be initiated for some years, and some strategies may even be dropped as God begins to shape the vision in the congregation. The primary job of this team is to research and create ideas for communicating what it discovers.

Preferably, as Teams One and Two do their jobs, the hearts of those participating on the teams become even more fervent for renewal and transformation within the congregation. As their passion grows, so will their communication with others. A grand by-product of this process is the creation of raving fans for the vision when the congregation is transformed by God's Spirit.

Team Three: Developing Personnel

Team Three consists of leaders whom the pastor recruits and trains to help implement change. A pastor should not recruit these particular leaders or potential leaders for Teams One and Two. The pastor will need all the leaders that can possibly be recruited for Team Three.

Team Three will likely start with a small number of people. However, if it fails to grow in size, the congregation will not become healthy. Growth is a sign of health. Growth in any congregation comes in proportion to the number of groups that are started and the number of new leaders that are recruited and trained. The pastor must start with those in the congregation who are already committed to a new mission and vision, regardless of whether they are now active or not. This group will grow only as the pastor and other lay leaders attract new people and recruit them to the team.

The pastor must meet individually with persons who have the potential for leadership, listening to the vision they have for their own lives. The pastor must then share his or her vision for the congregation and must try to connect this person's personal vision to what God wants to accomplish through the congregation in order to change a community. Inviting this person to be part of a new and growing team of people who will develop into future congregational leaders, the pastor promises that the time will not be wasted. If this person agrees to meet with the new group once a month, he or she will become better at leading in all aspects of life.

The pastor will then develop for the team a curriculum that focuses on two main topics: the development of healthy leaders and the development of healthy congregations. In first-person terms, this intimate commitment sounds something like this: "Healthy leadership means understanding that my salvation in Jesus Christ is a call to serve my God with the talents, strengths, gifts, experiences, and passions that God will continue to give me. The primary purpose of this service is for me to join God's mission in bringing women and men into a relationship with God. My role in serving God, whether as a parent, spouse, employee in the workforce, or congregational participant is a missional one. Life and fulfillment with God is found in losing or giving up my goals to join God's agenda in reaching this world. Through this kind of leadership, I find true joy and significance."

Pastors should teach that leadership is influence. As leaders, we serve by using our influence for God and God's mission. We serve to find the lost and to influence them to enter into relationship with the God who is beckoning. Servant leadership is not pandering to codependent consumers who want a god to suit their agendas; rather, it is serving those in need in order to reproduce new disciples who in turn will join God's mission.

During this training the pastor will teach that leaders are passionate, courageous, flexible, missional, wise, and positive people who take responsibility for leading. Pastors will also teach many of the skills attached to leadership—motivating, delegating, and accountability. They will teach leaders how to pray and develop the kind of character that makes them healthy women and men of God.

The pastor teaches this team not only about healthy leadership but also about the characteristics and functions of a healthy, thriving congregation. All healthy congregations are missional, just as all leaders are missional. True spirituality is being joined to God's mission, which is the same for all congregations. As wealthy cultures become increasingly pagan, missional congregations are always working within their cultures, cross-culturally. This means that leadership is required to guide congregations to adopt as their primary reason for existence God's mission of making disciples. As long as a congregation is primarily institutional in nature, serving consumer Christians as its primary purpose, that congregation (or denomination) cannot be healthy; the entity will cease to thrive.

The pastor then trains leaders to establish missional audits, determining how each of the congregation's ministries can be brought into alignment with the mission. If a ministry cannot be brought into alignment, it should be discarded. Failure to support the mission means that a ministry works against it, no matter how benignly.

The next step is to train about vision. A vision that is bigger than the congregation—a vision that takes on the entire community that the congregation is called to serve—will energize and produce excitement for the mission and its accomplishment.

The third step is to deal with both structure and authority. The pastor must show how all congregations, regardless of size, should be staff-led. A staff member is anyone who is provided with a responsibility, given the appropriate authority, and then held accountable for results. Being a staff member has little to do with remuneration, as volunteers often make great staff members. (Some congregations refer to paid and unpaid servants.) Authority, responsibility, and accountability should be married and not divided. A congregation handles authority by creating boards that govern, pastors that lead, staffs that manage, and congregations that actually do the ministry. (The book *Winning on Purpose*, by John Kaiser, © Abingdon Press, explains this entire process with detail, clarity, and humor.)

Book (handwritten margin note)

At some point, pastors should instruct these leaders that when systemic change occurs in their congregation, real values will surface. These real values are three in number: power, turf, and money. If the congregation becomes mission and vision driven, and the staffing and structure shift as described above, conflict will be generated. Do those who hold the power, control the turf, and direct the money do it for the institution (and ultimately themselves) or for a mission that focuses primarily on others who are not yet a part of the congregation? When the latter occurs, the congregation has moved from sickness to health.

Power / *Turf* / *$.* (handwritten margin notes)

During this training about healthy leaders and healthy congregations, the pastor shares the learnings of Team Two and the prayers of Team One. The pastor also uses feedback and input from Team

Three about how to implement strategies and tactics to communicate urgency and cast vision. The better the pastor communicates all that is occurring with each of the three teams, the better and more quickly things can change. Every time the pastor meets with one of the teams, he or she should give an update on crucial insights recently discovered by the other two teams. A pastor may tell Team Three what Team One discovered on their most recent prayer walk or describe a key way of communicating urgency suggested by Team Two. Obviously the pastor will want future leaders involved in praying for the vision and mission. Part of the training will be to let those in Team Three help the pastor develop an overall strategy to lead the congregation through the systemic change required for the transformational process to begin. Team Three helps implement all that is happening in Teams One and Two from a human perspective.

Team Three must be constantly growing. As new people come into the congregation, the pastor must select those God has gifted for leadership to be a part of this team. This team will be the allies when the pastor is leading the battle for systemic change. Therefore, the more these leaders can learn about developing influence with people in the congregation, the better. There will come a day when they will need to use that influence with great skill and wisdom. Additionally, the more leaders a pastor can get to take part in the formal leadership of the congregation (no matter how unmotivating that might be to her or him), the better. This way, the new officers have both a formal and an informal influence when the battle is joined.

Jesus said that no one builds a tower without first counting the cost (Luke 14:28-30). He also said that no king goes to war without adequate preparation and planning (Luke 14:31-32). No wise pastor attempts to lead systemic change in highly dysfunctional congregations (which describes most congregations in wealthy countries) without first counting the cost. The Church of Jesus Christ is littered with wounded, maimed, and dispirited pastors and lay leaders who tried to lead systemic change without understanding the severity of the battle and counting the cost of such an endeavor.

No meaningful, lasting, and substantive change comes apart from the Spirit of God. Our zeal, brains, and efforts fail without the Spirit's power. This is why Team One—the prayer team—is fundamental. It is foundational to all the pastor does. Without prayer, there will be no lasting change or fruit.

No one person is smart enough to think through all the issues related to creating compelling urgency, casting an invigorating vision, and crafting key strategies for their communication and implementation. The counsel of many advisors is necessary. This is the purpose of Team Two: to help the pastor think things through in order to avoid the "ready, fire, aim" syndrome.

All congregations grow in proportion to the multiplication of groups and leaders. However, leadership comes first because everything we do humanly depends on leadership. There will be no health, growth, and reproduction without the development of leaders, thus the need for Team Three.

True leaders will be the people who help the pastor lead change. These individuals will be called upon to stand with the pastor in difficult times. They must understand that the issue at stake is not a person or personality. The issue is God's mission for God's Church and how the congregation will either once again become involved with it or continue to ignore it and live with an inward focus.

Leading systemic change is a major, costly undertaking that many people will resist with awesome tenacity. The pastor cannot do it alone. The pastor needs God's resources, God's ideas, and godly leaders to see change occur.

CHAPTER SIX
Critical Mass is Critical

Barney disliked every pastor who came. None were as theologically conservative as he was, he thought they were all lazy, and no one had ever reached out to him. He always sat in the back row and often scowled, never laughing unless the pastor made a mistake. He was always asleep by the time the sermon started, except for the times he got so mad that he walked out of the service to go sit in his truck. His wife supported her husband but was embarrassed inside by both her husband's actions and demeanor, so she never said much to anyone. Barney was not one of the power brokers in the congregation because his behavior was too repugnant, but whenever the controllers had a disagreement with the pastor, they knew how to rile Barney up so he would take the offensive and conduct their dirty work.

Pastor Driscoll had been at his new charge for less than a week when Barney confronted him about his wife's dress and behavior. The pastor was clearly informed that his spouse was not honoring God and that, until she changed, Barney and those like him would never be able to listen to anything he preached, let alone follow his leadership.

Six months later at special foreign missions dinner, Barney upbraided the pastor in front of everyone, calling him a hypocrite. Allegedly, the pastor was talking about reaching lost people all around the world, yet the congregation, including the pastor, could not care less about the needy people who lived in apartments around the church building.

The following Sunday, Pastor Driscoll was preaching about love. As he rehearsed his sermon on Sunday morning, God's Spirit told him that if he could not love Barney and his family, then he could not preach on love. After wrestling with God for quite a while, Pastor Driscoll knew that he must seek Barney's best regardless of how Barney acted. The first thing he did before going out to start the service was to pray a blessing on Barney, his family, and his business. For some reason, Barney stayed for the entire service, even though he was asleep for most of it. As Pastor Driscoll moved to the back of the worship center after the sermon, he

stopped at Barney's aisle so he could speak to him before Barney did his usual end run out the side door. Pastor Driscoll shook Barney's hand and said, "Barney, it is good to see you this morning."

A year later, when Barney's wife was in the hospital, Pastor Driscoll came to visit. She asked if he still remembered the night her husband had embarrassed him. When he replied in the affirmative, she said, "You need to know that your action of shaking his hand and greeting him the next morning has changed his life. He really respects you now." Pastor Driscoll did not tell her how almost every day for the last year he had been praying for God's blessings to be given to Barney and his family. He just smiled and thanked her.

Never Take a Knife to a Gunfight

Getting ready for a battle is perhaps as crucial as fighting the battle. Although there have been times when warriors with fewer provisions and inferior equipment have defeated those with more resources and better arms, most wars are won by those with the most resources and well prepared armies. As stated previously, preparing to change the culture of a highly dysfunctional congregation is analogous to engaging another nation in battle. Because those leading are often unprepared, systemic change seldom occurs in most congregations.

First, the change agents have not spent adequate time creating urgency and casting vision. Neither task can be overemphasized. Some leaders may think that they have cast enough vision and created enough urgency, but most change experts realize that they have underestimated the task. The pastor and lay leaders nearly need to become sick of hearing themselves talk about vision and need. People either tune out what is said, or they have a difficult time understanding that they are the problem (individually or collectively). Many persons take a very long time to realize that their circumstances are dire and that there can be a better tomorrow. Most people need time to make the emotional transitions that signal loss of things they value.

Second, most leaders go into the battle without a big enough army and the required number of officers (leaders). It often takes several years of intentional input to have a big enough corps of leaders to tackle the engagement. Chapter 5 outlines the three teams a pastor needs to develop, and the third team must constantly grow in numbers. Failure to have enough leaders usually means that systemic change fails. Without a strong prayer team, all change is irrelevant, as God is probably not driving it.

However, creating urgency, casting vision, and having enough leaders (including key people praying) is still not a direct hit. Change is also a numbers game that involves people, dollars, and influence. This chapter is about planning and preparing for the campaign. The Old Testament describes God as having determined whether Israel would win or lose its battles. Still, most of the time, Israel had to engage the enemy in battle in order to win, and God often honored the strategies taken by David and other great warriors. The same is true in transforming congregations from dysfunction to health. Only God brings life out of death, but God does not usually bring transformation until God's people are praying, acting, behaving wisely, and willing to endure major suffering. Part of wise behavior is preparing for the battle that will come. Being content with an impotent, declining congregation that is ignored by the community is evil. When such congregations begin to reclaim their God given mission, there will be opposition, often from God's people, and we must be ready.

You Get No Credit for the Obvious

Dysfunctional congregations, regardless of size, expect the pastor to "do ministry" because, in the minds of most, that is what the pastor is paid to do. In this codependent culture, pastors are not often paid to equip others to do ministry, which is biblical. When pastors fail to meet the expectations of dysfunctional congregations, they begin to lose influence.

At the same time, healthy pastors must recognize that they do not gain influence by doing the expected. Doing the expected is similar to a child asking for an allowance for brushing his or her teeth. Most parents would say no to that request because all people ought to clean their teeth. Those who choose not to do so will usually suffer the consequences. Pastors who are preparing for a major change down the road cannot afford to lose any influence with the congregation when they are already at an influence deficit upon arrival. The basics must be covered. And yet maintaining the basic status quo is why changing it is so difficult.

First, a pastor must do the basics so as not to lose influence, while at the same time add to the job the casting of vision, the creation of urgency, and the development of three new teams who will probably bring no change to the congregation for the next three to five years. The pace is like working on a major home renovation project. Although tearing out walls, scraping old paint, ripping off faded wallpaper, and doing all the other stuff that creates a mess is an enormous amount of work, there are few tangible results.

Second, the pastor is now walking a fine line. While beginning to develop ministry teams that will pick up many of the ministry responsibilities expected of the pastor, the pastor must at certain times maintain a chaplain's touch. This helps the pastor not to lose influence and still to have some time to breathe, think, and prepare for change. At this point, it is helpful to find a solution-based mentor or coach who has been through the same struggles and can serve as guide to help avoid common mistakes.

The pastor will minister to many people because they expect it, but these same people will not necessarily support the pastor when conflict comes. From their perspective, the pastor was simply doing the obvious. The "doing ministry game" is one the pastor plays not to lose, knowing that in most cases it will not help him or her to win.

Therefore, the pastor must strive not to lose influence through failing to accomplish expected ministries during the process of preparing for systemic change. Gaining resources here means not losing potential resources. Those who end up with zero losses, yet no gains in basic ministries, have done excellently.

It Takes Money to Make Money

Everyone has heard of a person who becomes an overnight financial success. However, most people must begin to save a little here and a little there before they are ready to make investments that will produce a greater reward. Building resources while preparing for systemic change is more like saving than investing. Developing leaders is a crucial investment that will take time before a payoff. So the pastor and key lay leaders must now focus on building up their savings account, putting in small deposits over time.

There is one cautionary risk to this long-range approach that is a byproduct of the transitory culture in which we minister: We may build up a good savings account that often takes a hit because newly developed leaders and allies move. So part of our prayer life should develop confidence that God will help us keep the right people and that God will send us key people when the time is right. While we pray this way, we must work as though the leaders that God has sent will be with us for the long term.

One way that a leader earns capital is to be seen as a trainer and as one who makes disciples. Of course, the pastor should be the trainer of the three teams described earlier. But additionally, the pastor is also looking for others to train and to find training for. For example, a pastor who asks someone to take over the children's Sunday school should either provide or, in most cases, broker the proper training necessary to do the ministry well. It would even help for a pastor to go with this person to his or her initial training to help show that the pastor cares about the person and the ministry.

Even congregations that are not staff-led need to treat workers like valued staff. It's often the little things that mean a lot—a smile, a thank you, a nod, or a few words complimenting someone for doing an awesome job. Our pastors have found that taking one Sunday a year to recognize workers has paid great dividends and provided loyal workers who will serve well to achieve the mission. I am often amazed during congregational consultations when people tell me the pastor has no idea what they do, or wonder if the pastor even cares. If a congregation has committees, the pastor can ask to occasionally attend committee meetings and offer thirty minutes of training.

One way to deliver training is to e-mail materials or Internet links that provide insight into specific areas of ministry. If the pastor is seen as one who cares enough to take the time to e-mail a worker, that worker becomes a supporter of the pastor.

In one sense, preparing to lead systemic change is like running for political office. There is a need for voters. Election Day is analogous to Systemic Change Day, and until that day arrives a pastor is constantly convincing those in the congregation that he or she is worthy of their vote.

Inviting key people and forming a discipleship group is one way to build up the lives of those who will one day strongly support the pastor. Those who are invited need to understand that they are doing this to prepare for mission and that they will be held accountable to do ministry with what they are learning. At some point they will be expected to share their learning with others because the whole point of discipleship is reproduction. The pastor is training and mentoring so others in turn can follow that example.

Another way to save long-term capital is for pastors to model that which they want they congregation to produce. If you eventually want the congregation to focus outward, then you need to model how you reach out to others in evangelism and mission. If you want the congregation to become generous toward God with their income, then you will need to model for them how you give (even though your income may be less than many in the congregation). If you want them to become a praying group, you will need to model that you are a person of prayer. The congregation must see their pastor behave consistently in relation to his or her stated passions.

Now, few leaders are super-saints, but each leader has strengths. Therefore, be selective in the ministries that are credible to model. Do this by determining which ministries will motivate the congregation to join God's mission when the change comes. Also, let the congregation know that you are willing to go outside your comfort zone to join God's mission. I remember knocking at the door of an apartment to talk to someone about becoming a Christian. The deacon standing there with me said, "You know, I am with you here tonight because in a sermon you said you find this very uncomfortable, and I know you are just as scared as I am."

Effective leaders do not ask followers to go somewhere that they have not gone and would not go as leaders. This does not mean that pastors should spend all of their time functioning outside their giftedness. It means that they are willing to do anything to accomplish God's mission.

The pastor also makes deposits in the savings account by never conducting ministry alone. As much as is humanly possible, the pastor is always taking people into ministry opportunities so they can watch and learn how to get things done. This is how to train hospital visitors, assimilation teams, and prayer teams. A pastor who models, disciples, and trains is creating a corps of people that God will use to do even more ministry. This is a way to create spiritual IOU's. When conflict comes, these are the leaders who will be willing to follow, and perhaps even stand up and speak, because they know the pastor's heart and depth of integrity.

It Does Take Money, Really

In congregations today, real votes are not related to polity. People vote with their feet and their wallet. In congregations that are quite unhealthy and highly dysfunctional, people vote every week not to attend or not to attend the second time if they had the courage to come at least once. Visitors may not be able to articulate the underlying issues related to why they do not return; most simply know that this congregation is not a fit for the needs they and their family have.

Often the same kind of voting takes place when a pastor begins to lead systemic change. Many of the members who do not like or want the change may continue to come (at least they will not resign their membership). However, it is quite common for them to stop giving. They hope that the lack of income will discourage the pastor and make it difficult for the new changes to be implemented. This passive behavior comes from their perceived or actual loss of power in the congregation. Sadly, in many cases, their strategy works.

Systemic change often occurs when the congregation needs more money. Dying congregations usually have limited income because the number of people in attendance has been declining. Transformation usually requires new staff to provide administrative and management services for the new ministries, and new resources that help train leaders and the new disciples who are and will be coming. Too often, pastors who lead change find that once the new systems are ready to go, they have no funding for implementation and must cut dollars because disgruntled leaders are withholding their normal giving. This phenomenon requires planning so that the new momentum established with change does not quickly abate due to lack of funding.

That is why pastors should be gathering financial resources for the future during the several years they are preparing a congregation for change. One strategy is to approach those being trained and developed for leadership and specific ministries and speak to them about the future and giving. Some polities have grown so dysfunctional that congregational bosses can use accountability to prevent an outward focus on mission. If the current congregational bosses hold finances tightly in order to control the pastor, the pastor may not want to ask for money at this point. Rather, the pastor may ask emerging leaders on Teams One, Two, and Three to put some dollars, over and above their regular giving, into savings accounts in order to have funds available in the future to hire new part-time staff members or provide resources to develop new disciples. On the other hand, the congregation may permit the pastor to have a fund for future staffing, and these monies could go into it. Another option is to persuade persons to make designated gifts. However, the pastor needs to be careful that such gifts either are not manipulated by those running the congregation or are too restrictive in nature to be used when the time is right.

Pastors should be a part of civic groups where they can network and gain ideas about funding. Such contacts may lead to pursuing grants, special fundraising ideas, creating outside businesses that provide income, or even the creation of a 501(c)(3) to fund ministry ventures. Sometimes, people in the community will be willing to fund projects that they believe will meet felt needs even though such projects are conducted by a congregation that they do not attend, if they go to church at all.

The bottom line is that effective ministry requires the resources to fund it. Pastors who do not think about funding will often find themselves on the verge of great change and not be able to lead it due to the lack of money.

Pastors should also network with other pastors, schools, and para-church agencies to create a list of potential staff members to employ when the change comes. Congregations with solo pastors often need a part-time youth, children's, or worship minister quickly when the timing is appropriate. Many pastors who have not been doing the required networking to have access to potential candidates will lose momentum because it takes so long to find someone who will advance the change and help imbed it in the congregation's DNA.

There are many more large congregations today than in the 1980s. Often these congregations have people who are serving directly under key leaders but would like the opportunity to develop and lead their own ministries in some kind of congregational setting. Many smaller congregational pastors are not aware of who is available or do not even have access to other congregations because they have not been networking with the pastors of larger congregations. Therefore, even if they have the funds to hire part-time staff members, they do not have the names of people who are both qualified and competent. Obviously, if pastors recruit staff members in this way, they need to do so correctly and with integrity as they interact with pastors and leaders of other congregations. Many pastors of large congregations are happy to help those who are serious about transformation, particularly if such transformation will lead to making more disciples. This willingness to help is even greater in large congregations that have internship programs designed to develop ministry leaders.

Money and hiring the right people go together. A staff-led congregation needs both paid and unpaid staff members to make it happen. Therefore, when the opportunity to lead change comes, the leaders must be ready to move both financially and with the right personnel.

Another side benefit of networking with effective pastors in the area is to see how they do ministry in ways that are outside the box yet produce significant results. The benefits of networking are usually multiplied for the time invested.

It's Possible to Play with Fire and Not Get Burned

The Bible uses an interesting metaphor in dealing with enemies: "heaping coals of fire on someone's head" (Prov. 25:21-22). The concept is quite simple to explain and almost impossible to perform, especially without the help of the Holy Spirit. It means that we should do very kind things for our enemies in return for all the evil or mean things that they have done to us. This image will become learned behavior if the pastor and other lay leaders decide to seek systemic change within a congregation.

As the point of systemic change draws closer, some will work their networks diligently and forcefully to stop it. These people will be watching. As the pastor gains more and more influence and as more new people come, the congregational bosses realize that they will soon be outnumbered and outvoted, thus losing control. This realization will produce passive-aggressive and, in some cases, openly aggressive behaviors against the pastor and those perceived as the "pastor's people." The result often is that lines are drawn, and an "us versus them" mentality develops on both sides of the line. This is particularly true if there are phone, e-mail, and verbal campaigns waged to get people in the congregation to line up on one side or the other.

When this begins to happen, the pastor realizes there are enemies to the change. These enemies may be well-intentioned dragons, emotional terrorists, or just plain alligators. In some cases, they may function like King Herod with the wise men, saying that they are positively interested in what is occurring while intending to sabotage or kill the first-born offspring. In other cases, they make it quite clear that they do not like the direction in which the pastor is taking the congregation; therefore, they do not like the pastor and want him or her to leave. At this point the pastor must remember to be as gentle as dove and as wise as a serpent (Matt. 10:16).

Often during this phase God may give the pastor the opportunity to "heap coals of fire" on the heads of one or more of those opposing the change and acting in ungodly ways. In fact, it may be during a time of crisis that the pastor has the opportunity to go above and beyond what is expected in ministry to help an antagonist or an antagonist's family member deal with some major problem. Obviously, the pastor should serve not for personal political gain but because serving is the right and biblical thing to do. However, the pastor should be wise enough to note that this crisis may be preparing this person for a beneficial change. Often, the result of such ministry is that while the antagonist still may not approve of the change, he or she will no longer work at blocking it and will encourage others to act the same way.

As the time draws near for major systemic change, the pastor and other leaders must not get caught up in antagonistic relationships that may hinder the change. The pastor does not back down or back off from leading the change but rather engages the evil behind the conflict with all the spiritual and human resources possible. Our Lord often works to make change happen by doing things we do not understand until after the fact.

If You Can't Stand the Heat, Don't Redo the Kitchen

Many of the congregations in our region have gone through systemic change, and we continually work with others that are in process. The pastors who have led and are leading these changes are my heroes. They, along with their spouses and families, have paid a great price, and there is layer after layer of spiritual scar tissue under their skin. Our pastors work hard at being healthy leaders who lead healthy congregations.

However, I have been consistently surprised by how some of our pastors, along with others throughout the country, have reacted to the attacks and the severity of the conflict produced by leading such transformation. Perhaps many assume that if someone is truly leading the congregation to adopt God's mission, problems should not occur. Perhaps some believe that injustice should not take place when someone is attempting to do the right thing. Or perhaps observers do not believe that God's people can be so vicious.

We must understand that dysfunctional, declining, and ineffective congregations in an increasingly pagan culture is exactly what a culture of evil desires when the kingdom of God is breaking out in fresh ways. Leading a congregation to be serious about once again fulfilling God's mission is a major spiritual undertaking. This kind of decision will involve warfare that occurs in the heavenlies and is more significant than what happens here on earth. When Jesus instituted the Church, he did so in order that the "Gates of Hell might not prevail" against the kingdom of God (Matt. 16:18). Pastors and lay leaders of systemic change in congregations are involved in serious spiritual work. A study of Paul's letters, noting his comments on suffering, should cause us not to be surprised or shocked that suffering occurs. In fact, perhaps pastors should be pleased that for the first time in their ministries, they have the right enemies.

We must also remember that if Jesus died for the Church, which he established, then we as his followers must expect conflict when directing the Church to act like the missionary culture that Jesus requires. In wealthy nations, we may not experience physical death for our actions, but we should expect that the kingdom of evil will try to create as much separation from normalcy as possible if we live and die for the kingdom of God. Those who try to contain God's love for only their friends and families will make attacks on our integrity, our spouse, and our family. If they can cost us our jobs or negatively affect our employment, they will do so out of self-interest. Pastors leading change should remember that Peter lost his life for feeding sheep.

Therefore, do not go down this path of leading a congregation from dysfunction to health if you are not ready to work hard, perhaps lose the battle, and experience great pain in the process of winning. Of course leading dysfunctional congregations also produces pain, but it comes in smaller doses. Perhaps the most important way to prepare for change is to know ahead of time (for three to five years) that it will not come without great cost. And though one can prepare with this knowledge, the leader has no idea what the cost will be. Only the Lord knows. Therefore, the leader must believe that the Lord will give the grace needed to pay the cost. The leader must also take by faith that this risk is worth it.

This frank discussion of pain and cost is enough to dissuade most pastors from putting preparations in motion, so part of the pastor's preparation is to work at developing a support system for the family as well as to develop personal habits that are healthy and disciplined. Too often, pastors are loners, forgetting that ministry is to be accomplished in community. Finding community may mean paying for a mentor or a coach. It may mean developing relationships with other effective pastors in the community, even if they are part of a different denomination. The price of change will be high. The more prepared the pastor is to pay that price, the better.

No Pain, No Gain

My heart is warmed when I hear a pastor say, "I am finally getting to do the ministry I thought I would do before I went to seminary." Once systemic change has occurred and the new DNA is embedded in the congregation, the pastor's job is a whole new world of opportunity. The ministry takes on a positive note, there is affection for the work that the pastor does, the pastor's family is honored and supported, and the pastor has the opportunity to see most of the efforts of ministry producing fruit. It is a world in which one is privileged to equip, lead, and oversee a congregation that has joined God's mission.

Systemic change occurs as a result of hard work. Years of casting vision and creating urgency ad nauseum means working extra hard to do regular ministry while at the same time preparing new teams of people for the day that change will come. It requires planning ahead in terms of money and people. And it takes being willing to join the Lord of the Church in suffering to pursue that mission that Christ has for it. Not only is the gain worth the pain, the gain far outweighs the pain.

CHAPTER SEVEN
Can We Get Some Help Here?

Old First Church had seen its best glory days back in the 1960s and 70s. It had averaged over eight hundred in worship, moved to the outskirts of the city (relocating with plenty of land and a new building), was filled with seminary faculty and students, and was seen as a leading congregation in the denomination. But as it entered the new century, things were quite different. Average worship attendance was below two hundred and fifty, the formerly new building looked as old and run-down as it really was, the city had built around it and had put up signage that obscured the building, and the people had little hope for the future as a decline in numbers and dollars became the norm.

Pastor Ed arrived on the scene three years ago, and the church had begun to grow a little under his leadership. Still he found that change, even small incremental change, was hard to implement. He was able to spiff up the foyer so it looked like 1980 had arrived. But trying to get old, worn-out restrooms redone and restored was like pushing string uphill. Either the money was not there, or the time and motivation of those responsible for overseeing facilities was not there. Pastor Ed felt that he was doing the right things, but the leadership and the congregation could not get over the hump and create momentum. He could take three steps forward only to take two steps back.

Pastor Ed asked his denomination if he could get any help. They told him no because his congregation was the largest in the region. Their focus was on keeping most of the little congregations on life support. At least his congregation could breathe on its own.

Pastor Ed took a chance and asked a consultant from another part of the country, involved with another denomination, to come in and help him and his congregation. This decision was not easy because his leaders were not sure that spending money to do this was the wisest investment with so many other things that needed to be done. But Pastor Ed persisted, and his leaders agreed, more out of respect for him than in seeing the need.

Six weeks after the consultation was completed, the congregation was averaging over three hundred in worship, vision informed the decisions leaders made, things were getting accomplished, and the congregation had generated a list of people whom they were praying might become disciples of Jesus Christ. The congregation had moved from malaise to hope.

Outside Help Is Required for Most

The majority of congregations in wealthy nations are in decline or on a plateau. Many of these congregations were at one time healthy, growing, and doing effective ministry for those who attend as well as for those in the communities in which they exist. However, the opposite is now the case for most. There is little effective ministry occurring, primarily due to the fact that congregations are unhealthy and conduct community life in dysfunctional ways. Leading these congregations to experience systemic change is almost impossible, and most pastors, despite their desire, cannot accomplish the task by themselves.

Despite all the rhetoric, most congregations do not want to pay the cost of change. They usually want the results of change but are unwilling to do what it takes to get the results. The price is too high.

To begin with, nearly everyone in the U.S.A. (and in many other countries) comes to church as a consumer asking the question: "What will you do for me"? The consumer does not ask what he or she can do to help. The consumer expects to have expectations met; if they are not met, a consumer will either go somewhere else or will stop shopping. Consumers who are already in the congregation are not going to change to meet the needs of the consumers yet to come, as long as their needs are being met. Most small congregations are closed small groups. In these groups, social and some spiritual needs are met for those already inside, but there is little or no interest to reach out to those outside the group.

Another reason congregations do not want to pay the cost of change is that most believe God created the Church, and their congregation in particular, for them. In a culture that is becoming more and more pagan, many view their congregation as a weekly refuge from the world in which they live. They do not see their congregation as a mission outpost designed to reach lost people; rather, they believe it exists as a place where the converted may be safe from the larger, evil world.

Congregations are a refuge for lost people, and they should be a refuge for disciples who are hurting because of life's tragedies. But this is not their primary purpose. The best medicine for those facing hurt is to become involved in effective ministry. Too often, we become codependent with the wounded, telling them that they do not need to do ministry until they are healed from their emotional and spiritual pain. And to some degree, that advice is true. But hurting people should eventually get back into the race that our Lord has called us to run. In the running, hurt is often healed, when we are no longer focusing on our own pain but on the needs of others.

We spend so much money and time on health care and medication that a therapeutic bias emerges, and we begin to believe that we should avoid sacrifice and suffering at all costs. Making changes that inconvenience us and are done for others whom we may not even like or respect is not something we are inclined to pursue. Congregations made up of Anglo-Americans experience this withdrawal all the time, but so do ethnic congregations living in communities where the ethnicity has changed. They too will not often make the changes necessary to reach out to the new people living around them.

Many believe that change will make that which is comfortable, though not completely fulfilling, worse. An unknown future is more threatening than a somewhat comfortable, but not quite fulfilling, present.

These cultural reasons and more make leading systemic change almost impossible for pastors to pursue on their own. The challenge is particularly daunting when the congregation sees the pastor as a temporary alien, an invader within their culture who will be gone within a few years. Many competent pastors live under condemnation because of the incompetent pastors who came before them. The people often do not respect the newest pastor because they assume that any pastor is not worth following on such a risky journey.

Another major reason why most pastors cannot lead systemic change on their own is that God has not given them the gifts and talents to do so. In my experience of supervising pastors, perhaps 10 to 15 percent of pastors have the leadership skills required to produce such change, should God work through their ministry. A small percentage of pastors possess either a natural talent for leadership or the spiritual gift of leadership. Other pastors can increase their leadership behaviors, but without the gift or talent they probably do not have the innate resources needed for such a difficult task.

The good news is that most pastors, who do not have leadership talents and gifts, can learn and practice effectively the leadership behaviors that will prepare a congregation for systemic change. However, these pastors will need help—special help—when the time comes to produce the actual change.

During a time of systemic change, the pastor needs the skilled help of a denominational or outside consultant. This consultant must be competent and courageous and must understand the task at hand, which is to help lead the congregation through systemic change. Without this help, many pastors will probably not see systemic change take place.

Consultation Versus Intervention

In our region, we have seen some dramatic reversals in congregations that continue to this day. The most dramatic are three congregations that have grown from 70 in average worship attendance to 800-1000 in six or seven years. Many other congregations have grown from 50-150 in average worship attendance to 300-700, in the same amount of time.

I have personally seen this process work in other denominations, in numerous places in the U.S.A. and in other wealthy countries. Yet traveling though a number of these places, I have learned how other denominations have done and continue to do congregational consultations like the ones that we have done (see my book, *Hit the Bullseye*, © 2003 Abingdon Press), without the same results. I've pondered why and suspect that for the most part we did not conduct "consultations" within our region; we conducted congregational interventions.

Congregations that are healthy and on the upside of their life cycle do not need interventions. They are already effective and often need to learn how to become more efficient at reaching people in the community who need the transforming grace of God. Such consulting is more than tweaking the machinery of the congregation, but there is no need for major changes in the entire system or within most of the individual systems. It is more a matter of helping the leaders become better at what they are doing and, in some cases, helping them find more leaders or staff who will complement those already there.

Congregations on the downside of the life cycle are another matter. And the further down they are, the greater the intervention must be. In many ways, dealing with such congregations is like confronting an alcoholic. Everyone who cares about the person tells him that this is the last chance he will be given. At this juncture, those who care deeply point out the elephant in the living room (this person is a hopeless drunk), offering hope by confronting in such a radical way. Dealing with highly dysfunctional congregations that have been that way for a long time is like dealing with "old drunks." Pastors need to clearly articulate the severity of the situation while at the same time offer great hope if the congregation and its leaders will take advantage of the opportunity for change.

An intervention is different from a consultation in that the interventionist knows from the start that the job is to lead systemic change, helping to set aside the current system and replace it with one that is mission and vision driven. It often means devising strategies to remove the current congregational bosses from their positions and to replace them with those who are committed to a new vision and mission. It means interacting with the pastor to set up accountability structures that the pastor must meet as well as introducing a new system and sub-systems in which accountability is required for everyone. It means that by the time the changes are implemented, the congregation has started a new life cycle with a new vision and mission, the pastor is a leader held to high standards of accountability, accountability is part of the entire organizational DNA, and the right lay leaders (raving fans of the new mission and vision) are in the appropriate positions of authority.

Such interventions require those who have the skill and the courage to take on this major task. The interventionist functions as both a prophet and a facilitator, which is precisely why most pastors cannot lead systemic change. They typically cannot be the prophet and survive to lead the congregation into a new day. Many prophets get martyred in the process of bringing such news. Furthermore, many pastors need the help of a good facilitator to inform them about what needs to be done and in what order a systemic change occurs.

If the pastor has been engaging the tasks outlined in this book, the intervention will be much less confrontational than most of the interventions in the congregations within our region. The congregation will be much more open to a new vision and mission because their pastor has been constantly communicating urgency. Team One has been praying, and God will begin to show them miraculous answers to their prayers. Team Two has been developing strategies. Team Three has been growing and developing new leaders, and competent people are ready to populate the formal structure and lead the informal structure. There will still be conflict, but it will be more acceptable because of the preparation that the pastor has instituted.

Finding the Right Tools and Consultants

There are many tools available to congregations and consultants alike to help them gain an analysis of where a congregation is. Most of these tools are excellent at what they are designed to do, which is to provide analysis, but they do not help with interventions. These tools are like thermometers or stethoscopes. Although these instruments help doctors diagnose disease, they do not help doctors treat disease. Good doctors use all the tools they can. They realize that their responsibility is to take all the data and do two things: (1) provide a diagnosis, and (2) prescribe a course of action that will help the patient move from sickness to health, with the fewest possible side effects.

There are helpful consultants who develop their own tools, and there are weak ones who repackage tools that they have not used before. There are consultants who do well in certain specialties but are not as competent in other areas of consulting. Some consultants do well with helping healthy congregations or with helping congregations make incremental changes. But few consultants are skilled interventionists. Identifying these interventionists is difficult because some observers are not sure that performing interventions is the job of a consultant (or district superintendent, bishop, or regional executive).

Therefore, when a pastor has been preparing a declining, dysfunctional congregation for systemic change feels that it is time to implement change, that pastor needs to invite someone who is skilled at conducting congregational interventions to come in. If the congregation has a denominational or associational connection, preferably they will be able either to provide the person with or to sanction a consultant from outside their group. If the denomination is not ready to act in this way or if the congregation is independent, then the pastor should have the congregation hire the consultant. (This is another expense that the pastor should anticipate during the years of preparation.) A strong consultant who does interventions well can slingshot the congregation though the change process, saving a number of years of investment and thereby ensuring that the change will actually take place. Continued support by a competent outsider also helps embed and implement the new DNA even more quickly.

Intervention Model: Big Picture

The following model is one we have used extensively in my region, and it is one that I have used with congregations all around the world in various denominational settings. (As a side note, polity does not prevent a successful outcome; rather, polity means accomplishing tasks differently.) The model has two aspects. The first aspect is the "line in the sand" weekend. The second is a yearlong relationship with an outsider (the consultant or the consultant's designee) who meets monthly with the leaders of the congregation.

The "line in the sand" weekend event is like the initial meeting with the alcoholic during a personal intervention. In a dramatic fashion, the intensity of the drama depends upon how well the pastor has prepared the congregation and upon the number of dysfunctions within the congregation (the elephants in the living room) that require open and honest exposure. The drama includes confronting the people who are the "elephants" so the leaders can see hope for a better tomorrow. In many cases, the result at the end of the weekend is to present to the congregation its five greatest strengths, its five greatest concerns, and five prescriptions that require implementation within the next six months. The prescriptions address major systemic changes that if implemented will change the very nature of the congregation. These changes usually involve mission and vision, structure (because such changes will reveal the true values of the congregation), and distribution of leadership (empowering the pastor to lead, though with great accountability).

Usually, we ask the congregation to do several things, regardless of their polity. The first is to spend the next month in significant prayer about the prescriptions. Next, have a time when the congregation votes. If there is no such event, people often believe that nothing has changed. Finally, vote for or against the prescriptions as a whole because to pick and choose is to reject the vision and mission. (Picking apart the intervention is like taking only half of the antibiotic that a doctor prescribed, which means that the sickness will come back and will be more resistant than ever before.)

When the congregation decides to implement the prescriptions, the pastor and leaders are then committed to work with the consultant or the consultant's designee for a minimum of one year. This person will be on the congregation's campus at least once a month but will stay in touch with leaders throughout the month by phone and e-mail. This person will at times attend staff and board meetings, conduct training for new staff members, and help facilitate new ministry endeavors that focus the congregation on achieving the mission and advancing the vision.

As Tom Bandy (*Kicking Habits: Upgrade Edition,* © 2001 Abingdon Press) and other consultants have documented, congregations wanting to change must learn not only to create new habits of ministry behavior but also to stop following old habitual patterns. The yearlong contact helps the addiction to stop, because the facilitator must sometimes intervene by helping people to realize that the old ways of doing things are creeping back into the picture.

This year is crucial. Congregations only get one year, or at the most two years, to create systemic change. If the changes created during this time are not enforced, the congregation will fall back into old patterns of behavior and will be inoculated against systemic change for the next twenty years. Again, like treating alcoholism, the longer and more intense the rehabilitation is, the better chance that person has of not returning to the old patterns that created so much havoc in their life and the lives of those around them.

An Intervention Mode: Detail

The model described below reflects to some degree our polity (American Baptist) and the issues raised by it. However, adaptations can be made for different groups. I have consulted and used this model with over forty different denominational groups in various nations. This model also reflects how to implement change in a denominational setting. Congregations in more independent settings will probably need to contract this work out to competent consultants.

We have learned that when a pastor or congregation contacts us and states a desire to be healthy and grow, we need to talk to both the pastor (if a pastor is in place) and the governing board before we do anything else. In talking with the pastor, if we determine that he or she is the primary reason that the congregation is not growing, I ask whether the pastor is willing to resign. I need to know the pastor's commitment to this process and how many risks he or she is willing to take. If the pastor is not willing to risk, then the congregation cannot be asked to risk. This normally works not by actually asking for a resignation once the consultation is completed, but rather by setting goals and deadlines that will lead to resignation if they are not met. I believe firmly in giving pastors a realistic chance to succeed.

When meeting with the church board, I tell them that if they go through this process, many of them will probably need to vacate their positions because it has generally been under their watch that the congregation has declined. At the same time, I offer them hope that if they follow the methods and systems we suggest and use the tools we provide, they can again be a healthy, growing, effective congregation. So the question is: Do they want to hold to their positions and watch the congregation die, or do they want to see if God will again visit their congregation with life and health? Of course, the fact that we now have a proven track record often helps them chose to try and live again.

When the leaders decide to go through what we call a consultation (even though it is more than that), we ask them to complete a self-study. This is a brief document that elicits from the leaders all kinds of information about the congregation. It normally takes the leaders two to three months to get the data together. Some could finish the study much more quickly, but the time it takes to complete the work is often in proportion to the level of dysfunction. They must send the completed self-study materials, along with all documents from the congregation, to the consultant at least two weeks before the "line in the sand" weekend event takes place.

In congregations with solo pastors, the weekend begins on Friday afternoon with a two or three hour interview with the pastor. If there is any staff (even part-time), we start on Friday morning so that all staff members can be interviewed. Following the interview with the pastor, the consultant has dinner with the pastor and the pastor's spouse in order to interview the spouse and ask questions of the couple.

Next, we conduct a focus group on Friday evening with a cross section of the congregation (twenty to thirty people). I ask the pastor to introduce me and then leave. No other leaders should be present. I ask three key questions of the group:

- What do you like about your church?

- What would you change to improve your church?

- If finding enough money and the right people is not a problem, what do you want your church to be or look like in the next five to ten years?

I spend six hours (9 AM to 3 PM) on Saturday with the pastor and key lay leaders. During this time, I ask the lay leaders the same three questions, provide an analysis of the congregation (often dealing with the elephants in the living room), provide training on what a healthy congregation looks like, and offer an initial evaluation of strengths, concerns, and prescriptions. (The description of a healthy congregation is found in *Hit the Bullseye* and will also be updated in the next chapter of this book.)

On Saturday afternoon and evening, I write the report that will be given to the congregation on Sunday. I e-mail the report to the pastor and then meet with him or her early on Sunday morning to get feedback and make any changes if necessary.

On Sunday morning, I preach a vision message, encouraging the congregation to be open to taking risks. After the service, during a meal, I present the report to the congregation. Every person gets a copy. The report includes the key five strengths of the congregation, the five biggest concerns, and five prescriptions that are sure to address the concerns while building on the strengths. I then take questions, after which the weekend part of the consultation/intervention is over.

The prescriptions often relate to having a day of prayer in which the pastor and lay leaders lead the congregation in prayers of confession for failing to fulfill God's mission. There is usually a prescription to have the leaders make a conscious decision to focus the congregation outward in terms of its mission. Next, there is a prescription for developing a vision.

In light of our polity, we have a prescription where the people vote to put in abeyance for three years those parts of the bylaws that dictate how the congregation conducts its ministries. This allows us to help the leaders create a new board, which has a different role, and to help the congregation become staff-led, which introduces a high degree of accountability. The last prescription may relate to the facilities, how funds are to be used, or the hiring of part-time staff members. Each of these prescriptions has a deadline, usually within the next six months, and they must be accomplished within the prescribed times.

We also set goals for the pastor. Pastors in our region are expected to be in pastoral clusters. We often get them a coach as well. And we have them set goals for how they will specifically accomplish certain things by the end of one year.

Then, in our setting, a facilitator or consultant who is part of our region works with that congregation for a year. This person is involved in training many of the new staff, getting resources to the leaders, and so forth. One key element is to go to board meetings every so often to make sure the new board is governing, not managing or leading. The consultant functions as a facilitator, an encourager, and a prophet, when necessary.

The result of using this model, with required variations for different situations, is that a majority of our congregations have gone through transformation. Many of them are still on that journey.

One Crucial Caveat

Another benefit derives from this model by dealing with a problem that, while affecting few congregations, is major when it appears.

Some congregations are led by abusive pastors. *Direct Hit* assumes that most unhealthy congregations are in a cycle of decline because of incompetent and/or untrained pastors and laity who want to control the congregation out of their need for significance rather than to focus outward. However, some growing and non-growing congregations are led by pastors with poor personal wiring who use their position to rule over people. These types of pastors gain personal significance more from control than from leading and serving.

These pastors often build their empire under the guise of deep spirituality. They often use the Bible and privileged "God talk" to cower lay people into submitting to their wishes, regardless of whether such wishes produce health and growth or greater dysfunction. These pastors do not want to be in mentoring and coaching relationships where their personal issues will be exposed. The last thing they want is to be held accountable. In our model of ministry, while the laity turns over the leadership of the congregation to the pastor, the pastor turns over control of the ministry to people. Abusive pastors cannot handle this well.

Our model of working intimately with both pastors and lay leaders brings to the surface many of the more prominent issues that some pastors face. This allows us to intervene in behalf of the congregation and get help for the pastor when possible. It also enables us to have the relationships required with congregations to help pastors exit well. Because of good relationships, congregations are open to letting us assist them in finding a new, healthier leader.

Everyone Can Use Some Extra Help

Although most pastors can develop the required leadership behaviors to get a congregation ready for systemic change, the majority do not have the gifts and tools that are required to lead the systemic change alone. They need help. When competent people give this kind of help, it is amazing to witness the transformation that can take place.

This offer of intervention is one of the two key roles that denominations should be performing. The other is to help congregations reproduce and create new congregations. People yearn to see their denominational leaders as key allies in helping congregations to grow and be transformed. Pastors are desperate to see their denominational executives as resources and allies in leading transformation. We in denominational life must be willing to function as prophets as well as facilitators of health and growth. When such intervention occurs, then denominations have value because they help pastors and congregations reach beyond themselves to reproduce new generations of mission-minded leaders.

CHAPTER EIGHT
It's Time to Really Move!

Like many recent graduates, Pastor Hamilton does not have a lot of options. That is why he and his spouse now live in a very old community where he is the pastor of a congregation that has been in existence for more than one hundred years. The building, an historic landmark, is well kept, and the three hundred seat sanctuary provides plenty of room for the twenty people who gather for worship each Sunday. Also like many rookies, Pastor Hamilton has no idea what to do or how to lead this group of people whose only vision is to keep this historic institution alive. But Pastor Hamilton has one unusual thing going for him: a denominational leader who is willing to take a risk and try an experiment with the pastor and the congregation.

The denominational leader asked an interventionist to come in and conduct a consultation with the congregation. This same person also assembled a group of pastors interested in health and growth, and invited Pastor Hamilton to participate each month. Both the leader and Pastor Hamilton see each of these tactics as something that might work, while realizing that they might also fail in trying something new.

The interventionist came in for a weekend consultation, with the agreement that the denominational leader would continue to work with both the pastor and the congregation in a consistent manner for the next year or longer. During that weekend, the consultant raised discussion about several elephants in the living room. The people wanted to control their new pastor because he was inexperienced. They could not trust him to make sure things did not get worse or to maintain the building well. The people said they wanted growth but did everything to mitigate it. And finally, there really was no hope that this congregation could once again become alive and vibrate. The consultant, while dealing with the dysfunctions, offered these people and their pastor hope if they would be willing to take some risks and begin to act quite differently. They found a workable balance in being honest about the problems, offering major systemic changes that demanded risk, and raising new hope. The pastor and people agreed to try a three-year experiment to see if things could change.

Two years into the experiment, the congregation has almost tripled in size, averaging in the mid sixties in worship attendance. During that time, six new disciples have committed themselves to Jesus Christ. The congregation once again regularly sees children and younger families in their midst. And there is great hope that all the new things God is doing are just the tip of the iceberg. The congregation once again focuses on the future far more than the past.

Leverage the Intervention

The pastor and lay leaders may have spent three to five years conducting incremental changes while preparing for the day that systemic change arrives. The intervention is the beginning of a brand new day. If the congregation adopts the prescriptions and is willing to risk, the pastors and those leaders that the pastor has been developing must move from first to third gear. This is not always easy to do because often pastors have created wise habits of moving slowly to implement smaller incremental changes. However, assuming the pastor has been preparing the congregation for change and the consultation has been an intervention, it is time for the pastor and new leaders to move rapidly. Anyone who objects to the increased pace can blame it on the consultant and intervention.

It is now time to create a new DNA and embed it in the congregation. This requires quick action after the consultation and a tenacious commitment to new behaviors that reflect the new DNA for a minimum of five years. Habits are difficult enough to change aside from replacing old DNA with new. The intervention should start a new life cycle for the congregation. If such is the case, it functions like the birth of a new congregation. When new babies are born, they require a lot of care and attention, taking up large amounts of time to ensure that they survive long enough to begin life well and healthy. A good intervention is often the closest we can come to the church building burning down or relocating to another place in the community. These types of events often cause a congregation to make many changes that help it start over again with a new sense of mission and vision.

Warning Label

This chapter requires a warning label for the church leader. If the intervention works well or is accepted by the congregation, the pastor and leaders should move quickly to make all the changes they can possibly make in a short amount of time. Because the window of opportunity is quite narrow (one to two years maximum), this brief chapter packs a big punch by describing all the things that need to occur. Compressing so much advice may be overwhelming to pastors or church leaders and may even be so discouraging that some will never attempt to lead systemic change.

So as you read, remember that you will have had three to five years to prepare for these days. I am telling you ahead of time the cost, so you can be making preparations. Also, you need and can work through all of this with a consultant or facilitator. Those who have a mentor or coach should realize that the pastor and the mentor or coach form a team. The pastor is not in this alone, trying to juggle multiple balls in the air.

Running With Purpose

If Team Two has done its job well, the pastor by this time should have a clear statement of the vision for the congregation, along with major strategies for how to implement this vision. The intervention should have settled once and for the next ten years (until the next intervention is needed) the mission or purpose question. The leaders are committed to an outward focus, recognizing that the congregation's primary reason for existence is to make more disciples for Jesus Christ. If the vision is a description or idea of how an outward-focused congregation will change the community, it is time to step up the communication of vision.

Stepping up the communication of vision may sound as though it is impossible if the pastor has been communicating vision ad nauseum for the last several years. But now is the time to tie together the vision and mission, roll out key strategies that have been developed, and make sure that the new vision statement appears on everything the congregation has in print. In fact, this would be a good time to change the congregation's public appearance in relation to letterhead, signage, newsletters, and more. The images that people see should reflect a new beginning and rebirth of this congregation, with a new purpose and an exciting, compelling vision. In some ways, this step is similar to a store going out of business and reopening under a new name, with signs announcing new management and the offering of goods and services to a whole new clientele.

This may also be the time to spend money that has been saved on painting and renovating rooms in the church facility. Actions like this provide tangible short-term wins that help the pastor and leaders gain credibility for even more important decisions related to change. They provide a more welcoming environment for people to invite guests. And they outwardly state that this congregation is once again on the move.

A second thing leaders should do quickly is to begin a ministry audit of all the ministries of the congregation. The purpose of the audit is to decide which ministries support the new mission and vision, and which ministries do not. Those that do not fit must be changed or discarded. It is a challenge to discard any ministry, particularly if that ministry has been effective in the past, but the best chance that the leaders have to accomplish this feat is immediately following the intervention. The test of whether or not the mission is what drives a congregation is not only what the congregation initiates but also what it stops doing. Additionally, having the ability to decide helps to solidify the new leaders as leaders. Some people may not like what the new leaders have done, but even those individuals recognize that the leaders are acting, and many will see that their actions are consistent with what is being said.

A third thing that must be accomplished during this first year is the establishment of new leaders for the congregation. (Note: These things are usually happening simultaneously rather than in sequence. This is another reason why the three to five years of preparation are crucial). Structure never changes first. If the primary focus is on structure, all changes will be like lightening rods that attract chaos from those wanting to stop change. However, if a congregation is going to implement a new mission and achieve a new vision, then the structure must change. Congregations within various polities will need to figure out how to restructure, but they must do so. Congregational structures reflect how the three basic values—power, turf, and money—are handled. Congregations must use money to resource the mission and enhance the accomplishment of vision. They must use facilities as missional tools to make the new changes into reality. And they must give the power to lead and make decisions to those who are committed to having an outward-focused congregation. If the structure does not allow these shifts to occur, then the new DNA will not be embedded, the momentum created by the intervention will be lost, and the last three to five years will have been a "learning experience." This is the time for the pastor to leave and try again elsewhere.

The new structure will be configured distinctly in a variety of congregations, depending on local context and denominational polity, but the results of each configuration should be the same. Authority, responsibility, and accountability should be married. This means that the people who have responsibilities are given the required and appropriate authority to carry out those responsibilities and are held accountable for fruitfulness in their ministries. Rigorous accountability should be introduced throughout the entire system so there is clear evidence that the mission is or is not being accomplished.

It should be obvious in the new structure that staff members lead the congregation, whether they are full-time, part-time, or unpaid servants. These staff members oversee the basic ministries of the congregation and are held accountable as individuals for how many disciples will come to Jesus under their ministry, how many leaders they are developing, and how their particular area of ministry will grow during the year. Staff members will be honored and rewarded if they achieve their measurable goals; they will be asked to step down from their positions if they do not meet their goals on a consistent basis. Obviously, these understandings have been worked out ahead of time, and staff members have been given ample opportunity to practice working in this new system.

Another result of the new structure, regardless of configuration, is that the new board no longer manages the ministries of the congregation or attempts to lead it. The board governs. The pastor is the leader who is responsible for the overall ministry and effectiveness of the congregation. The staff members, who are hired, terminated, and work for the pastor, manage their particular areas of ministry. And the people of God (laity) are equipped by the staff members to *do* the work of ministry. In some polities that have personnel committees (or staff-parish committees), these committees generally hold the pastor and staff members generally accountable (performance reviews and new hiring decisions). This type of committee is a workable forum to handle the performance accountability of the pastor. (Note: Many of these committees contain or represent the power bosses who render the pastor impotent as the leader of the congregation by managing or interfering with the paid and unpaid staff that the pastor should be leading. During the intervention, and when it is time to change the DNA and restructure, this barrier is often one of the elephants in the room that must be identified.)

The pastor and the consultant or the facilitator, assuming they are two different people, should decide who will be on the new board and who will be the staff of the congregation. Board members should be chosen from those leaders who are committed to the new mission and vision, are financially supporting all that is occurring, and are already involved in ministry. New board members do not sit on the board to represent any group in the congregation or any special interests or agendas. This new board should only number between three and five people, regardless of the size of the congregation, because its primary responsibility is to govern. In some polities, this reduction in the size of the board will meet enormous resistance because many have been trained to believe that broad representation on a board is the same thing as actually leading and doing ministry. Although the goal of diversity is a crucial aspect of the outward-focused DNA in a mission-driven congregation, focus the drive for diversity on broadening leadership of these new ministries to persons who are not yet part of the congregation. The key role of the board is to hold the pastor accountable for goals and to make sure the pastor does not violate the boundaries that the new board has set. This new board needs strong people who will protect the pastor and the staff members, while functioning as their best cheerleaders in producing needed changes. It should also be a buffer between the pastor and those in the congregation not overly excited about all the changes.

Too often, pastors want to put all the best leaders on the board. The problem is that these leaders may be among the best staff members. It is the staff who will lead, manage, and develop the ministries that will implement with vigor the new mission and vision of the congregation. At this point in the life of the congregation, staff members are more important than board members. Although the pastor wants and needs wise people on the board, the best leaders should be on the new staff.

The pastor should look at the fundamental ministries that people expect when they come to church and should make sure the best people for those tasks are leading as staff members. The pastor should be very clear about the responsibilities each staff member has, helping to develop behavioral goals and specific performance goals for which staff will be evaluated.

All staff members must accept three major goals. The first goal is the number of new disciples that will be brought to Jesus under their respective ministries. Setting this as the primary goal makes outward focus everyone's responsibility, from the person leading the nursery staff to those responsible for assimilating new people. It also creates an environment of outreach that leads staff to be creative in reaching new people, whether adults or children. The second goal is the number of new people that each staff member will train to be involved in his or her ministry each year. Congregations grow in proportion to the number of leaders and groups that are developed. The third goal is specific numbers or percentages by which that staff member's ministry will grow during the year. Almost no one is exempt from these goals.

There are one or two rare exceptions to the three major goals. In a staff-led model, staff members who work for the pastor now oversee the facilities and the finances. Obviously, the staff who hold these two positions will find it difficult to meet the evangelism goal. Therefore, they must team with other staff members to help them achieve their evangelism goals. For example, the financial person may develop some kind of training dealing with debt or investing that the small group person can use as an outreach tool with new people. The facility person might team with the assimilation person to creatively use the church campus to reach out to new people. The people leading these areas should be developing other leaders to help them, and need to set goals to expand what it is they do.

The first six to twelve months after the intervention is crucial to the systemic change that needs to occur in most congregations. The importance of this time period is also why years of preparation and planning are so important. The better prepared a congregation is and the more planning that has occurred, the better the chance the congregation has of making the change. If the pastor has implemented well the strategies laid out in *Direct Hit*, the pastor is now established to lead for the next five to ten years, to enjoy the fruits of the past labors as well as the type of pastoral ministry that God intends.

It is important at this juncture to recall that often when new pastors come to dysfunctional congregations, they try to change the things that can be changed only through an effective intervention. They try to change these things with no preparation, inadequate prayer, and a lack of leaders committed to the direction in which they want to take the congregation. This impatience is why many pastors fail. They do not understand the difference between *preparing a congregation for* systemic change and *leading a congregation through* systemic change when the time is right and the spiritual and human resources required for the difficult journey are in place.

For example, in our congregational circles, many pastors believe that if they can just change the structure, often by changing the bylaws (which means circumventing denominational polity in other traditions), they can be successful. They believe this because the congregational bosses know how to expertly use both the formal and informal structures of the congregation to stop what the pastor is called to do. Pastors think that if they can just get control of the organization, all will be well. Nothing could be further from the truth. The issue is not control (although it will be at some point). The initial issues are lack of mission and vision, lack of leaders, lack of followers, and the lack of knowledge to know how to address all these deficits.

A New Congregation, A New Job

A new congregation means that the pastor now has a new job description. The pastor's new role centers around leadership rather than chaplaincy, and the pastor should take up this new role as diligently as possible in the first few months after the intervention. It is a key ingredient to the change. The people must begin to have different expectations of who does ministry and how it will be accomplished.

The pastor is now expected to lead the congregation. First and foremost, the pastor is the congregation's spiritual leader. It is the pastor who stands as God's representative each weekend, communicating clearly and relevantly God's mind from God's Word to the congregation. It is the pastor who calls the people to prayer, fasting, humility, and acts of compassion when appropriate. It is the pastor who has that special word from God in times of individual, congregational, or national crises. It is the pastor who models, speaks, and motivates others to implement the mission and fulfill the vision. It is the pastor who (with biblical and theological support) reminds the people that the new ways of acting are a result of the congregation again joining God's mission for the Church. It is the pastor, along with those responsible for worship, who plans creative, relevant, interesting, and meaningful worship services. The pastor then vigorously critiques or evaluates those services to meet the deep needs of believers and potential new disciples alike. The pastor finds authority for other acts of leadership as a result of serving as the ordained, spiritual leader of the congregation.

The pastor is now the leader of the well-formed organism called the congregation. Thus the pastor is the keeper of the mission and the caster of the vision. The pastor must not allow anyone or any ministry, no matter how appealing, to deter the congregation from its mission to be focused outward. Once a congregation has made the decision to move outward in mission, the pastor must not make the mistake of thinking that everyone will support the decision or that even those who voted for it will know how to live it out. The primary impetus of the Christian culture is to move congregations inward. Christian consumer demands cause congregations to be insulated. Fears of compromise and having unsavory or inappropriate dealings with non-Christians (simply because of how we assume they might dress or act, or what questions we think they might ask) move congregations inward. The daily business of leading a healthy congregation, which is producing effective ministries, causes the congregation to move inward. The pastor needs the wisdom that best comes from godly mentors and coaches, and the iron will that best comes from the Holy Spirit, to keep focused on the main thing. No one will protect or desires to protect the mission in the way the pastor should. Failure on the pastor's part in this outward focus means that eventually all the hard work and success will be lost.

The pastor now moves to a higher level of casting vision. The vision and mission can be tied together, and the pastor should be able to demonstrate how new strategies and reached goals are beginning to make the vision and mission a reality. The pastor should create new urgency and vision calendars, articulating how to communicate urgency and vision to the congregation every Sunday in ever more demonstrable and interesting manners than in the past three to five years. In the first two years after the intervention, it is crucial to explicitly tie everything to the mission and vision. Do not assume people are making the connections because most are not (and many new people are arriving). The pastor needs to do it for them repetitively and with great creativity. For example, the pastor becomes the collector and teller of stories about how God is working in new ways throughout the congregation. The pastor continually walks around to find people who are implementing well the mission, and, with great delight, tells their stories to everyone. These stories are told and retold as the pastor continually casts vision. Again, no one else has the platform that is available to the pastor to cast vision. And usually, no one will take the responsibility to cast vision as often or as well as the pastor can.

The third main task in the pastor's new job description is to develop leaders. This should not be a new responsibility if the pastor has been following the prescriptions in *Direct Hit* and has been preparing the congregation for change. At this point, however, the pastor works with three groups to develop leaders: (1) the new staff, (2) the board, and (3) people whom the pastor and other staff members are recruiting from those who are new to the congregation.

The pastor should meet with each staff member to find out his or her needs in terms of responsibilities, goal setting, and accountability for meeting goals. If there are common needs, the pastor can deal with them during the training he or she now conducts in each and every staff meeting. The pastor can provide personal training in areas of expertise and become the broker in other areas, bringing together the staff member and the needed resources. The pastor should do group training (staff meetings) in two major areas: leadership and congregational health. The pastor should also provide training for some staff members who must train and develop the leaders they are recruiting in their respective areas of ministry.

At this point, the people realize why pastors must turn over much of the ministry to the laity. Pastors of healthy, growing congregations have a whole new set of tasks. If these pastors are still expected to visit all who are sick, meet with all who are hurting and needy, and go to every meeting, they will have no time to do what they should be doing. However, it is the pastor's responsibility to make sure that the congregation is meeting these needs—and is meeting them better than the pastor alone could do. The pastor and the staff can create teams to actually do many of the ministries that most congregations expect their pastors to do (such as hospital visitation, contacting new people, or conducting premarital counseling).

The pastor also trains the board. Each board meeting, like each staff meeting, has a training component. The pastor should train board members in what it means to govern. The pastor should help board members to understand leadership and to know the characteristics of a healthy congregation. The pastor trains board members to train others to become board members in the future. Again, the pastor provides expertise whenever possible and at other times acts as a broker, bringing in the needed human resource to conduct whatever training he or she is not yet equipped to provide.

The third group that the pastor trains are those who are new to the congregation, who have the potential to be leaders and can help the congregation implement the mission and achieve the vision. The pastor may meet with some of these people individually or collectively on a quarterly basis. However, the pastor is always creating a pool of new leaders to help advance the congregation in joining God's mission for the Church.

Another of the pastor's main tasks is to be the primary fundraiser for the mission and vision. Thus, the pastor takes seriously the need to regularly and consistently preach regarding money, the use of personal and collective finances, and the need to financially support God's mission. This means looking for those in the congregation whom God has blessed with financial resources (or the ability to consistently generate such resources) to challenge them about how to get involved financially and to use their talents to raise dollars for God's kingdom more than their own. The pastor understands that being the primary caster of the vision means being the primary fundraiser for that vision.

As with dollars, the pastor is the primary recruiter for the vision. When casting vision in sermons, the pastor challenges the congregation in positive and relevant ways to join God and use their gifts and talents to build up the Body of Christ numerically and spiritually. Thus the pastor and the staff members develop key strategies and tactics to recruit teachers, small group leaders, assimilation team members, and others. The pastor then leads at the macro-level to help implement these strategies.

This new job description also requires many pastors to learn how to preach in new ways and how to develop a leadership lectionary around which to plan sermons. This new way of preaching entails learning how to tell stories, incorporate more and more stories into sermons, and develop sermons by using "story structure" instead of outline structure (see *The Homiletical Plot*, by Eugene Lowry, © 2000 Westminster John Knox Press).

The pastor as leader and preacher will also become an expert on media and the use of media in sermons. Younger generations no longer sense that books or print provide authority for why things should be embraced. These generations view the screen as an authority that shares visibility with the pastor and addresses what should be embraced. Many pastors must learn how to speak and motivate a group by being positive, telling stories, and being an authentic and transparent leader. Often, we need to go outside the life of the church to gain a critical appreciation for how speakers in the political, business, and entertainment worlds motivate and lead. While we may not buy into many of the concepts that they espouse, we can learn from their methods in order to use the pulpit to lead people individually and collectively to embrace God's mission for the Church to reach this world.

The pastor as leader will determine what topics should be addressed every year and when is the best time to do so. The following topics might be on the list:

- The mission
- The vision
- Urgency for the mission and vision
- Values and behaviors
- Key theological and cultural issues
- Strong biblical teaching for belief and action
- Finances
- Service and mission
- Evangelism
- Discipleship
- Dealing with complex family issues

Many models for preaching present the pastor as a chaplain or a professor. But the model of the pastor as a leader, mobilizing a group of people to achieve a mission and accomplish a vision, demands an adjustment to the methods and content of preaching. Preaching is a difficult task that becomes even more difficult when the preacher realizes that God expects him or her to lead, using the pulpit as a place from which to rally the troops to take on God's mission. At a minimum, this shift raises the level of persuasion and response in the preaching event, transcending the type of sermon that merely informs.

Leading change is a difficult and risky task. The more one is alone in attempting this task, the greater the challenge. Those who possess excellent leadership talents and gifts usually make it happen, under God's good hand, because of their unusual gifting. Most pastors are not stars with special charisma but, rather, are ordinary individuals whom God calls to lead dying congregations to rise up and fulfill God's mission for the Church. When these pastors are on their own, with improper training for turning around a congregation, regardless of where they went to school, the task is almost impossible. This fact is proven again and again by the number of small, ineffective congregations and discouraged pastors in this nation and in other wealthy nations.

While recognizing that the task is difficult, *Direct Hit* is an attempt to offer hope to pastors and leaders of congregations that have lost their outward focus. Attempting and failing is much better than existing as a victim of the system.

For many pastors, failure can also mean losing a job. When appropriate accountability systems emerge in a region, it can even mean losing a job in those highly connectional denominations that have awesome unions for guaranteeing jobs to those who are chaplains maintaining dying congregations. Yet even with a safety net, trying and failing is better than being in a dead end profession where the essence of laughter is attending pastors' meetings to find ironic delight in grousing about a congregation or the ineptness of a denomination.

Direct Hit offers hope that it might be possible to try and succeed. Because if you succeed, you find ministry a delight that passes all others as God uses you to lead an effective congregation in changing a community and reclaiming lost souls for God.

Preparing for systemic change and actually leading systemic change are two very different things. Intentional preparation may take five years, particularly if you are on your own. However, if the time is right and you get the right help, the preparation can reap awesome temporal and eternal dividends for you, for the congregation, and most of all for the inbreaking kingdom of God in a very troubled world.

Ready. Aim. Go for it!

Appendixes

The Congregational Self-Study

We have used the Congregational Self-Study document with all of our congregations that have gone through our consultation (intervention) process. We use this document to gather data in preparation for the weekend event. We ask congregations to get the data and the documents required to complete the self-study to us two weeks before we spend the weekend with them. This allows us time to study the material and, if needed, request other data that may have been missing in the materials sent to us.

Leith Anderson and his staff at Wooddale Church created the Congregational Self-Study document several years ago. Wooddale has used the self-study extensively in mentoring other congregations. When Leith and I created the Teaching Church Network, we gave the document to other congregations to use with congregations whom they would mentor. As a result, hundreds of congregations have been exposed to the self-study in preparation for a consultation, an intervention, or a mentoring experience with a larger, more effective congregation.

There are a number of editions of the Congregational Self-Study. Mentoring congregations or other groups, such as our region, have often changed some of the questions to meet our needs.

This study and report should be created by a group of staff and leaders. All material should be stored on computer with widely used software and printed out in a notebook. It is preferable to have the entire staff and board involved in compiling and discussing this information.

History and Description

Write a brief history of your congregation (maximum four pages). Include those events that contributed to periods of growth or decline in the number of people participating. Write in a factual style. Avoid the temptation to puff the story for public relations and the temptation to inject personal commentary regarding past problems.

Provide a list of all full-time and part-time program staff positions for the last twenty years, or from the beginning if founded more recently. List schools and degrees for full-time program staff. Give the dates for staff tenure, and state the real reason why individuals left. (Leave out the pertinent specifics only where required by law.)

Provide a list of all persons who oversee specific areas of service. List the number of positions for which they are responsible in their oversight. State whether these persons are full-time, part-time, or volunteer staff.

List dates and provide descriptions for any building construction, major renovation, land acquisition, or leasing of facilities. List the amount of acreage you own, lease, or rent; the square footage of building(s); and number of parking spaces (distinguishing between off-street and street parking).

Write a summary of your congregational structure, including the individuals or groups who are responsible for program decisions, budgeting and financial oversight, buildings and grounds, and any other major interests of the congregation. List committees, task forces, program teams, etc., and explain how these relate to boards or councils. Provide a chart that reflects your current organizational structure.

List any formal ties or major informal ties to other organizations or associations. State how the congregation views and interacts with such groups.

Demography

Prepare a chart and graph for each of the following items for each year over the last twenty years, or entire history if founded more recently:

1. Number of members (if applicable) or regular participants (if no members exist)

2. Average attendance of your weekly worship services

3. Average weekly attendance of all your groups and classes combined

4. Number of persons transferring in to membership or regular participation

5. Number of persons transferring out of membership or regular participation

6. Number of baptisms

Estimate the average age of the persons participating in the regular activities of your congregation. State how this was determined.

State the percentage (a ratio) of persons who attend your worship services and who also attend some group meeting such as a class, support group, or service team. Count each individual only once (regardless of the number of additional meetings attended).

Prepare a list of the number of current members or regular participants who got involved:

• Prior to 1960

• From 1961-70

• From 1971-80

• From 1981-90

• From 1991-2000

• From 2000-present

List the total receipts and total expenditures for each of the last twenty years or for your entire history if founded more recently.

Without listing names, state the amount given by each of the top-ten contributors of record in the last fiscal year. Total these amounts and state the percentage of giving this total represents in relation to total contributions.

State the same information for the second ten contributors of record.

State the total number of contributors to the congregation during the last fiscal year and the average amount given per contributor during the last fiscal year.

Community Study

Write a brief overview of the area and community in which the congregation is located or which the congregation serves.

This overview should include approximately one paragraph on each of the following features:

- History
- Population
- Income levels
- Education levels
- Social, ethnic, and religious diversity
- Age distribution
- Growth/decline trends
- Other characteristics you deem significant

Briefly describe the square mile that surrounds the primary location of the congregation.

Beliefs and Practices

List the core values and/or basic beliefs of the congregation.

List other important commitments or practices that characterize the congregation, such as:

- Covenants or Codes of Conduct
- Key social issues
- Political positions

- Regular activities
- Significant financial commitments

Documents

Please send one copy of this self-study in typed form one month prior to the assessment visit.

Please send copies of the following documents (if you have them):

- Articles of Incorporation and Bylaws (or "Constitution")
- Doctrinal statement
- Last two annual reports
- Last two annual budgets and financial statements
- Sample bulletin and/or newsletter
- Any policy statements
- Other printed documents you deem helpful in providing insight into your congregation

Self-Study Group

After the self-study information has been compiled and before printing the results in final form, the board and staff need to discuss as a group the following questions pertaining to congregational conditions. (In smaller congregations, gather twenty to thirty leaders, whether in official positions or not, to fulfill this requirement).

Please include the general consensus on each of these discussion questions in the report. Be sure to give the date when this discussion took place, and list those involved in this meeting.

1. What are the three greatest strengths of this congregation, listed in priority order (greatest strength first)?

2. What are the three most significant weaknesses of your church, listed in priority order (greatest need first)?

3. What three changes would you like to see made in your church, listed in priority order?

4. Do the leaders want this congregation to grow significantly?

5. Are the leaders willing to make the difficult decisions required for change and growth?

Church Life Cycles

I created this handout to use with congregational leaders when conducting our weekend interventions. I have also used it extensively in seminars designed to train pastors, lay leaders, and denominational personnel. This one handout contains all the essentials required to produce a healthy congregation.

As the document states, I am indebted to George Bullard for much of the work he did to apply the Life Cycle concept to congregations. This handout is a recent edition that draws upon helpful changes suggested by Greg Wiens, the state pastor for Florida with the Church of God, Anderson.

Introductory Ideas

George Bullard breaks the life cycle of a congregation into ten distinct periods:

Upside of Life Cycle	Downside of Life Cycle
Birth	Maturity
Infancy	Empty Nest
Childhood	Retirement
Adolescence	Old Age
Adulthood	Death

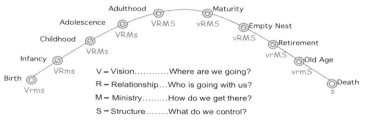

Life Cycle Of A Church

Adulthood   Maturity
Adolescence   VRMS   vRMS   Empty Nest
Childhood   VRMs   vRMS
Infancy   VRMs   vrMS   Retirement
Birth   VRms   Old Age
Vrms   vrmS   Death
   s

V – Vision............Where are we going?
R – Relationship...Who is going with us?
M – Ministry.........How do we get there?
S – Structure........What do we control?

Most congregations do not perfectly fit Bullard's categories. However, one category usually predominates, which enables a congregation to determine its current life cycle status.

Congregations on the upward side of their life cycle can reach their peak and start down in seven years or less. This rapid movement occurs due to living in a culture where, unlike the past, change has become the norm.

Highly dysfunctional congregations (those that have been on the downside of their life cycle for a long time) usually need time to prepare to create a new life cycle. This preparation time can take from one to five years, but once it begins the congregation probably has no more than two years to make the systemic changes required to start a new life cycle. It may take another three years to solidify the systemic changes that have been introduced. The preparation for change and the change process can be accelerated with outside help from either a denomination or the establishment of a mentoring relationship with either another congregation or consultant.

Congregations reaching the peak of their life cycle (adulthood) cannot stay there for more than three to five years without beginning to decline. Such congregations need to create a new life cycle while they are at their peak.

Preparing Congregations for Major Transition

Pastors need to create a great sense of urgency while at the same time cast a compelling vision. The purpose of creating urgency is to make the status quo unacceptable. The purpose of casting vision is to paint a picture of a preferable future. These two concepts are the negative and positive foundation for fundamental change. Failure to cast vision while creating urgency makes it nearly impossible to prepare a highly dysfunctional congregation to be open to change.

While creating urgency and casting vision, the pastor needs to be creating and discipling three groups. The first group is those who will pray for the congregation to become outward-focused, willing to take responsibility for changing a community. The second group is the initiators who will help plan the change process. The third group is the leaders who will help the pastor lead the change when it comes.

While creating urgency, casting vision, and developing the three groups, the pastor also works at developing a coalition of people who will be open to following the pastor's leadership when the change begins to happen.

Once these things are in place, the congregation is ready to begin the change process to create a new life cycle for the congregation. This juncture is the best time to enlist outside assistance to facilitate and accelerate the change process.

Creating a New Life Cycle

Bullard states that there are four key issues that determine a life cycle: **vision, relationships, ministry,** and **structure**. When **vision** and **relationships** are driving a congregation's agenda, the church is on the upward side of the life cycle. When **ministry** and **structure** are controlling the agenda, the church is on the downward side of the life cycle. When all four of these issues are at their peak, the congregation is at its peak in terms of the life cycle. Therefore, it is important to understand what is involved in each of the four issues.

1. Vision: There are three major elements that relate to Bullard's use of the term vision: *mission, vision, and values.*

MISSION: Mission is the bottom-line reason why a congregation exists. The mission is to minister primarily to those within the body, minister primarily to those not yet within the body, or do both. If the last option is chosen, then the congregation must prioritize those outside the body when it comes to the overall ministry of the congregation. This then focuses the congregation outward. CONGREGATIONS ON A DOWNWARD LIFE CYCLE DO NOT

CHANGE THEIR LIFE CYCLE UNTIL THEY BECOME FOCUSED OUTWARD!

VISION: Vision describes the results when the mission is successfully implemented. The vision must always be bigger than the congregation, describing how the congregation will change the community in which it exists. Vision produces passion for ministry. A COMPELLING VISION OFTEN MOTIVATES A CONGREGATION TO MAKE THE CHANGES NEEDED TO MOVE FROM A DOWNWARD LIFE CYCLE TO AN UPWARD ONE REFLECTING NEW HEALTH.

VALUES: Values are the boundaries that guide the mission and form the parameters for the vision. All congregations have values. The question is whether the values reflect an outward or inward focus. NEW MISSION AND VISION INITIATIVES ARE NOT ACCOMPLISHED WITHOUT THE ADOPTION OF NEW VALUES CONSISTENT WITH THOSE INITIATIVES.

2. Relationships: The ability for people to develop relationships with other people is crucial for changing the life cycle of a congregation. We must remember that people are not looking for a friendly congregation. Rather, they are looking for a congregation where they can make friends. If people cannot quickly develop meaningful and sustained relationships, they will not stay or be attracted to congregations. Small congregations are only friendly to those who are already a part of the congregation. Large congregations grow large because people can easily make friends on their terms. There are at least five key concepts that are crucial to relationships as this term is used in regard to life cycles:

- SATURATED AND UNSATURATED RELATIONSHIPS: People are like LEGOS™ in that they only have so many pegs to connect with other people. Therefore, they can have only a limited number of meaningful relationships. That is why new people must constantly be connected with people who are relatively new to the congregation.
- THIRD PLACES: Everyone needs a place where they are accepted or valued as a person for who they are, not what they do.

- GROUP DYNAMICS: Different size groups meet for different purposes. These purposes cannot be interchanged.

Large groups:	Unity for worship and mission
Mid-size groups:	Fellowship and teaching
Small groups:	Intimacy and accountability

- TRANSITIONS: People do not resist change, which is what occurs in organizations when they move from a downward life cycle to an upward one. People resist the loss of what was comfortable, provided status and influence, and made them feel significant. Understanding transitions enables change agents to identify that loss, develop plans to deal with the loss, and validate the grief that goes with the loss. *Transition plans often enable change to occur with a minimum of resistance.*

- UNDERSTANDING YOUR NICHE: Local congregations do not minister to all the variety of groups of people in the community. That is why God has placed a number of congregations in one community. The Body of Christ is comprised of numerous bodies in order to reach a variety of people. Therefore, each congregation must understand the mix (gifts, talents, abilities, backgrounds, etc.) that God has provided to reach different kinds of people. It also means that each congregation must study the people groups God has prepared it to reach in order to maximize its effectiveness. Growing congregations think like missionaries. Healthy congregations are always removing cultural barriers and building cultural bridges to people in order to reach them.

3. Ministries: The purpose of ministry in a congregation is to help disciples mature and to aid disciples in the making of more disciples. Therefore, ministry must meet people's needs and contribute to the growth and health of both individuals and the entire congregation. In missional congregations, ministry that does not grow must either be changed or eliminated. Therefore, there are two major questions that constantly need to be asked of all ministries in a congregation:

1. *How does this ministry contribute to an outward-focused mission?*

   Does it attract new unchurched people?

   Do the people leading this ministry understand its strategic significance, and are they intentionally designing it to reach people?

   Is this ministry growing?

2. *What is the strategy that underlies all of what we do with our ministry?*

   Do our ministries reflect missionary thinking?

   Are we willing to start with people where they are to move them to where they should be?

   Are our ministries growing?

One Model of Ministries

<u>Why</u>? Convert consumers into committed disciples of Jesus Christ
<u>Which ones</u>? Meet culturally determined ministry expectations
  • Worship and Music
  • Relationships/Groups/Friends
  • Care: Newcomer care/Member care
  • Family needs: infants, children, youth, adults
  • Education: training and personal development
  • Preaching
  • Well-kept facilities
  • Financial stability

Leadership Development

<u>How</u>? These programs meet the expectations of people (missionary thinking).

These programs must occur as they are culturally determined.

These programs are staff-led (staff may be volunteer, part- or full-time).

4. Structure: Structure (management) is like a skeleton in a body. If the skeleton can be seen, then the body is in trouble. Yet without a skeleton, the body will collapse. In healthy bodies, skeletons grow and develop so the body can grow. For any congregational structure to be effective, three major things must happen:

1. The leader must be growing and developing as a leader while developing more leaders.

The growth of any organization is in proportion to the leaders being developed within the organization.

The pastor usually works with three groups in developing leaders; the staff, the board, and key people in the congregation.

Without intentional leadership development, the congregation will not experience sustained healthy growth.

2. Leadership always marries three terms that reflect how work gets done, and those terms are: responsibility, authority, and accountability.

Responsibility means that there is agreement among the leaders on:

What the mission of the congregation is, and

Who is charged with specific tasks to see that the mission is implemented.

Authority means that there is agreement about:

Where the boundaries lie that create freedom of movement to perform the tasks.

Accountability means that is agreement as to what will happen to whom

When tasks are accomplished or not accomplished.

(**NOTE:** Groups do not lead, and groups cannot be held accountable; therefore, the focus is always on individuals to lead and to be held accountable).

3. The pastor/leader must turn the ministry of the congregation over to the laity (equip the saints to perform it),

and the laity must turn the leadership of the congregation over to the pastor/leader.

The pastor leads the congregation to implement the mission and accomplish the vision.

Staff members lead their ministries and manage the programs to produce healthy, growing disciples and, in turn, a healthy, growing congregation.

The board governs through policies and, therefore, does not lead or manage the ministries of the congregation. Rather it holds the leader accountable for the accomplishment of the mission.

BULLARD LIFE CYCLE – Adapted by Paul Borden and Greg Wiens

	Vision	Relationships	Ministry	Structure	Emotion	Behaviors	Issues	Needs
Birth Vrms	Dominant	Happens unintentionally	Only what is necessary	Informal	Passion	-Est. long-term vision -Est. evangelism and growth philosophy -Est. leadership style	-Can founding pastor stay? -Will lay leadership style change?	Make relationships intentional
Infancy VRMs	Dominant	Begin strategic implementation	Only what is necessary	Informal	Passion	Developing patterns of inclusion	-Clear values -Worship style -Lay mobilization	Quality ministry
Childhood VRMs	Dominant	Happening, though not the focus it once was	High energy in implementation	Based on leaders' personalities	Excitement for the long run	Focus on development -Staff -Ministries funding	-Future staff -Focus: children under 18 -Facility needs	-Quality and quantity -Establish structure
Adolescence VRMs	Dominant	Refocus on meeting needs qualitatively and quantitatively	Refinement and further development	Lacks: -Precision -Order -Consistency	Excitement for quality and quantity	-Staff development -Facility needs -Develop management systems	-Competition for future agenda -VR vs. PM	-Management systems -Leadership development
Adulthood VRMs	Dominant	Produces: -growth -commitment	-High quality and quantity -Community known	-Formal system in place -Functions well	-High morale -Sense of vision/mission	-Integrated systems -Facilities complete	-Few realize at peak -As good as it gets	-Change (new vision)

Maturity VRMs	Assumed and becoming lost	-Less new people -Disciple-making strong	-High quality and quantity -Community known	-In charge -Conserving the great tradition	-Feel good -But congregation passive	-Finances high, but over-budgeted -Worship great -Membership tenure high	-Lack of focus -Less new people -Congregation aging	-Re-envision -Diminish structure -Re-engineer
Empty Nest VRms	-Lost/missing -Loss affects most systems	Happening, but not keeping up	-Begin disintegration -We try harder	-In charge -Focus of the organization	-Denial -Nostalgia -Turning to anger	-Blaming -Issue is more commitment -Lack confidence with leaders	-System functions -Severe conflict	-Re-envision -Develop new ministries -Diminish structure
Retirement VrMS	Lost completely	Long-term members no longer invite people	Try new ones to fill the church	Overly managed	-Despair -Disappoint-	-Ministry changes -Want new workers -Won't confront -Want church to bury me	-Change may cause split -Change to create past	-New vision -Diminish structure -New relational form -New ministries
Old Age VrmS	Gone	Dormant	Failed	Total control	-Fear -Perhaps bitterness	-Structure focuses on chaplain ministry -Member gifts crucial	-Focus on member anniversary/ funerals -Structure kills any creativity -Congregation at rest	-Diminish structure -Create new ministries -Re-envision
Death S	Gone	Lost	Failed	Orchestrate an orderly transition	-Numb -No positive emotions	-Closure -Transition -Celebrate the past and close	-Complete closure -Resurrection in another form -Resource new ministry	-Transition for a new ministry

Stump Speeches

When serving in our region as the Director of Church Planting, Dr. John Kaiser asked me to speak to our new church planters about preparing Stump Speeches to continually cast vision for new congregations. I had talked about this for years, getting my ideas from the business guru Tom Peters. I created this handout for that event. Because I believe that pastors working to lead transformation must cast vision as much as, if not more than, new church planters, I have included this for your help.

Terms

Mission: Mission is the answer to the bottom-line question as to why your organization exists. It presents the ultimate purpose for being.

Vision: Vision is the description of a preferable future in five to ten years if your mission is accomplished. The vision must always be described in bigger terms than the organization. Vision must be described in both general images and specifics instances. It is the emotional fuel that motivates people.

Foundational Principles: Foundational principles are truths that are transferable across cultural, social, and even denominational divisions because they reflect ultimate truth. These principles are the foundation for mission, vision, values, structures, and behaviors.

Strategies: Strategies are broad ministry initiatives required to accomplish the mission and achieve the vision.

Tactics: Tactics are specific behaviors and programs that implement the strategies.

Alignment: Alignment means that there is consistency between the foundational principles, mission, vision, strategies and tactics. Be sure not to confuse principles, strategies, and tactics.

Concept

The concept of a stump speech comes from the writings of Tom Peters, who says that all good leaders have and constantly communicate their stump speech. Effective leaders can communicate it in three minutes or three hours. Good leaders can be awakened at 3:00 AM in the morning and start giving their speech. It becomes the message of the leader and is, in essence, how the leader communicates the vision of the organization.

At some point, we have to sit down and think through who we are, what we are about, and how we are going to implement our mission and achieve our vision. We need to work on both the concepts and the communication of this speech.

In most instances, people will want the Reader's Digest version of the speech. This means that we must learn how to communicate in a way that gets at the essence of mission and vision, offers the broad strokes of strategies, and suggests just enough tactics to give people some of the "how to."

Start With Mission

A good understanding of mission defines who you are as an organization. This means that you understand what you are and what you are not. Understanding who and what you are determines what you will do and what you will not do.

Move to Vision

Once you know who and what you are and what you will and will not do, you must then think through what you want to see accomplished, if you are successful in implementing the mission. You need to imagine how this will impact people and communities of people. This involves thinking about who you will reach, how many you will reach, and the particular niche you wish to achieve in your community. The more precise you are about these targets, the better you will be at communicating your message.

Develop Strategies

Once you know where to start (thinking through mission) and where you want to go (thinking through vision), then you are ready to develop strategies. Strategies will help you think about how to move from where you are to where you want to go. A good place to start in developing strategies is to think about what resources you currently have and what resources you will need to develop. The primary resources available to us are the Holy Spirit, people, money, and time. The leader's health, energy, talents, and family are also resources.

Next, you should develop strategies in relation to the environment in which you are going to be working to implement the strategies. National forces affect this environment. Local factors affect it even more. And then there are the factors related to your personal wiring and the group's DNA.

Finally, you should develop strategies in relation to the larger group with whom you are working.

Once you develop strategies, you should not change them without a good deal of thought; sometimes it may be tactics that are not working. However, strategies are not absolutes. The issue is the appropriate contextualization of the message.

Create Tactics

Take each of the strategies and develop key tactics that will show how that strategy is going to be implemented effectively. Tactics should be written in such a way that they can be easily evaluated as effective or ineffective. You will probably have several layers of tactics for each strategy. In most stump speeches, you will offer only the top layer. Some tactics may also help you achieve aspects of multiple strategies. Remember, tactics will often change; some will be discarded in favor or more effective ones.

Have Fun With Your Imagination

In personal terms, think through what will happen to the people and communities if all the strategies and tactics work. Visualize how the lives of persons and communities will be different because of what you and the people with you are accomplishing. Draw parallels from your experiences or from others' experiences. Create potential stories of what you expect to happen.

Preparation

Stump speeches are a vision-casting tactic, and there are four key components to casting vision. First, you cast vision primarily by telling stories, telling stories, and telling more stories. Therefore, a leader must become both a good storyteller and a collector of stories. Collect your own stories and the parallel stories of others. The stories should be positive accounts of how individuals enhanced a mission and vision.

Second, you cast vision by being positive. You are always helping people see what they can become rather than reminding them of how they have failed. Part of the leader's job is helping people see their own preferable future. You should convey any negativity in private, and you should do so only after you have done all that you can to lift a person up through positive affirmation.

Third, you cast vision by painting the goal for the entire group, rather than for individuals. Pastors must constantly be helping people to see what they can accomplish as a community of people. In our preaching, we must always ask the "so what" question of any biblical passage in terms of what the group will do or become.

Fourth, you communicate vision every time you talk to an individual or have the opportunity to speak or write to a group. Leaders must embody the vision, live it, and constantly communicate it.

The Speech

Start by preparing a fifteen-minute speech. It really does not matter where you start, because the speech must fit your personality. You can start at the end and work backwards or structure the speech chronologically.

The ingredients of a good speech:

- Create a need for people to listen by being specific and getting them to feel the need. Remember to have a main idea. Make sure that in your speech you briefly explain the idea, spend a lot of time helping people believe it, and spend an equal amount of time showing them the implications of why this vision should be implemented.

- Do not develop more than two or three key strategies. The idea is not to give someone the whole presentation in fifteen minutes. Touch only on the key tactics that help someone see how this idea is going to be implemented effectively.

- Think of yourself as a persuader. A good stump speech is trying to make converts even out of those who think they are with you. You should be enthusiastic and sold on what you are doing. People and their finances are attracted to those who believe that they are going to make a difference. People give and are recruited to vision, passion, and need.

- Tell as many stories as you can about the people whom you are going to reach and those that have already signed on with you. Tell stories that get people excited about what God is doing.

- Finally, describe the future in terms of specifics. Talk about what is going to happen in the lives of people, the way a community is going to be changed, and how individuals will think and act differently.

Communicating the Stump Speech

Once you have your speech ready, you should practice, practice, and practice some more. Try it out on a number of people. Let people give you feedback about where they got excited, bored, or confused. Every time you give it, note how individuals or audiences respond in certain ways. See where there is laughter, tears, or looks of boredom.

When you are comfortable with the content and communication of the speech, analyze its parts and presentation. Note where and how you talk about your mission, where you give vision, and where you discuss strategies or tactics. This allows you then to use the speech in flexible ways for different situations or audiences.

God has called us to lead people to a preferable future as committed disciples of Jesus Christ. I believe that this tactic of a stump speech is crucial to all we do as leaders in casting vision for a worthwhile mission. It is one of the fundamental ways we lead.

Training Church Boards and Staff

Once a congregation begins to turn around, pastors need to be training leaders. In particular, they should be training their new staff members and their new board members first. To answer the question, "What do we do?" I created these handouts to offer specific examples of what pastors can do in the training process. All pastors, in my opinion, should be training their staff and boards.

Training Church Boards

CHARACTER ISSUES:

1. Adopting the church's values as their own values:
   - Outreach: What are they doing in relation to their situation to implement this value in their life and the life of the church?
   - Intimacy: How are they practicing this value in their own lives and that of their family?
   - Priority of mission: How are they demonstrating that the church's mission takes priority in their lives, and how are they communicating this to others?

2. Personal spiritual development:
   - Prayer: individual and corporate
   - Bible study
   - Giving
   - Making disciples

3. Relationships:
   - Developing a relationship with God
   - Developing a relationship with their family
   - Developing a relationship with each other as a team of leaders
   - Developing a relationships with believers and unbelievers

LEADERSHIP ISSUES:

1. Developing their leadership skills, abilities, and talents
2. Developing other leaders. Each board member should be developing one person or a few people to be leaders in ministry and/or others to be new board members.
3. Encouraging their pastor and staff to continue to develop as leaders

ORGANIZATIONAL ISSUES:

1. Do they understand their role as leaders of the organization? Can they make the appropriate distinctions between policy and implementation, authority, responsibility, and accountability, and can they keep issues separated from emotions?

2. Do they understand that they are stewards, not owners, of the organization, including the vision, mission, and values? Do they know when and why to be firm and when to release control and be flexible?

3. Do they understand the difference between fairness and justice?

4. Do they know when to implement policy and when to make exceptions?

5. Do they realize that they are to hold the pastor and the staff accountable for the vision, mission, and values, while at the same time serve as the chief cheerleaders and protectors of their leaders?

6. Are they willing to stop triangulation in the church in dealing with issues?

7. Are they willing to confront as individuals and as a group? Are they willing to invest their social capital to stand up for the pastor and staff?

8. Are they willing to be trained to understand the future and its impact on the organization?

9. Do they think in terms of systems and how systems interact with each other to impact the organization?

PERSONAL ISSUES:

1. Do they have a feel for their gifts, talents, abilities, and temperaments?

2. Do they understand how each person's background, experience, personal wiring, and more enable him or her to fulfill different roles on the team and carry out different responsibilities?

3. Do they understand how their family systems have impact as individuals and affect the way that they function individually and in groups?

CORPORATE/COMMUNITY ISSUES:

1. Do board members think corporately, recognizing that they are responsible for the entire community of people called the church and that they must act not in terms of what is best themselves, their friends, or their vested interests, but in terms of what is best for the community?

2. Do board members understand the culture of the church, the culture that the church is trying to reach, and the culture in which they live and breathe nationally?

3. Do they recognize the need to be interdependent with other churches? Do they know that they are in the kingdom of God business, not their own local church business?

4. Do they understand how to market the church to the community? Do they know what their niche can be in becoming involved in the fabric of the community?

FINANCIAL ISSUES:

1. Do they understand the difference between current and deferred giving?

2. Do they know the difference between cash flow issues and debt?

3. What is their attitude toward debt?

4. Do they understand that staff should be viewed as a financial investment and not a liability?

5. Do they understand how land, facilities, and neighborhoods fit into the mission and vision of the church?

Training Church Staff

Working with individual staff members

1. First interview of the year:
   - Ask their dreams and visions for that year.
   - Share your dreams and visions for that year.
   - Discuss what will need to happen in their areas for such dreams and visions to occur.
   - Demonstrate how their goals and visions will impact others.
   - Share your expectations of them as a staff member:
     They are to achieve their goals.
     They are to be on time for meetings.
     They must meet with you individually at set times.
     They must participate in meetings and in ongoing ministry.
     They must develop as individuals.
   - State that your goal is to help them achieve their goals.
   - Discuss what needs to occur for them to develop personally and in ministry.
   - Discuss their prayer needs for themselves, their family, and their ministry.
   - Set the time for the second interview to discuss their goals for the year.
   - Spend time in prayer.

2. Second interview of the year (the primary purpose of this meeting is to lay out goals for the year):
   - The goals must be specific, measurable, challenging, and realistic.
   - Discuss time frames for meeting the goals.
   - See who needs to be recruited for their ministry in order to reach the goals.
   - Suggest resources for their ministry.
   - Confirm times and dates for future individual meetings.
   - Spend time in prayer.
3. Future individual meetings with staff members:
   - Go over goals.
   - Work on personal development.
   - Pray together.

Developing staff meetings for a year

1. Spend the summer laying out the schedule for the year.
2. Determine the areas in which you want to do training, i.e. Leadership, Organization, Big Picture, Character, Team Building, Added Value. Consider the following specific topics:
   - Developing mission and vision for individual ministries
   - Working on relationships
   - Recruiting
   - Developing teams
   - Risk taking
   - Mentoring individuals
   - Creating systems
   - Delegating
   - Managing resources and people
   - Accountability
   - Staff development

- Sharing the church's mission and vision
- Communicating the DNA of the church
- How staff communicate the DNA
- Spiritual mentoring
- Integrity
- Spiritual disciplines
- Developing a theology of ministry
- Team-building exercises
- Integration issues for major events
- Case studies
- Personal development

Lay out the agenda for the year

Meetings should be varied, however each meeting should include some of the following:

- Coordination of calendars and events
- Evaluation
- Best practices shared by different individuals
- Staff training each other
- Staff development
- Personal development

There are times that common experiences should be shared.

- Use tapes.
- Summarize books.
- Make notes on articles.
- Bring in guests who are experts in certain areas.

A Sample Month

Below is a sample month (calendar) that illustrates how to plan to communicate urgency, cast vision, and train Team One, Team Two, and Team Three.

FIRST SUNDAY OF THE MONTH

Creating Urgency: On Sunday morning as people walk into the worship center, they see pictures of the congregation from years ago. The title on the display is "Our Church Twenty Years Ago." The presentation is simply older pictures of the church showing Sunday school rooms filled with children, a worship center with most of the pews filled, Sunday school picnics with many children and adults, people being baptized, infants being baptized or dedicated, teenagers on mission trips, etc. Those who see the pictures are gently reminded of the glory days of the congregation.

Casting Vision: During the children's sermon, gather the three or four children around you on the steps to the platform and interview them, asking them what they think about God, the Bible, and living for Jesus. After they leave for children's church, tell the congregation how over the last three months two new children have joined the Sunday school and three have given their hearts to Jesus. Then tell the congregation that you can envision the day again when the dozens of children will be roaming the building each Sunday and twenty or thirty each year will give their hearts to Jesus. Show enlarged photographs of the five children that you have just mentioned, and state how these children are only the beginning of a new long line of children who will follow in their footsteps.

FIRST SATURDAY OF THE MONTH

Meet the three members of your new prayer team (Team One) at church, not at the regular hour of 7 AM for prayer but at 9:30 AM. Today, the four of you are going to the center of your town, and each one will walk a mile by himself or herself around the main shopping area. Instruct them to look at what people are doing, say hello to those they know, and observe all that is happening as people interact and do their shopping. While they are walking, they are to be praying silently that God will open their individual eyes to needs that their congregation will perhaps be able to meet one day. They are also to pray that their congregation will one day have enough health and strength to reach out and address the needs God reveals to them.

SECOND SUNDAY OF THE MONTH

Creating Urgency: Prior to the announcements in the worship service, interview a middle school teacher who may attend your congregation or who may be a friend of someone in your congregation. In this prerehearsed interview, ask specific questions that allow the person to share their concerns about the students he or she teaches. You might ask what the teacher has observed about the family backgrounds of the students, reading or study skills, drug use, how students conduct themselves in relation to sexual morality, etc. After this brief, five-minute interview, pray for teachers, the schools in your community, and the students who are living in such a difficult environment.

Casting Vision: In your sermon on the family and related issues, make one major point of application where you describe God using this congregation to provide coaching and mentoring for middle and high school students Tell about how older people will one day be helping students from difficult family backgrounds learn to read and study. Predict that this congregation will once again be filled with teens because people in the congregation are showing them the love of Jesus Christ by helping them in school.

SECOND SATURDAY OF THE MONTH

Meet with your prayer team (Team One) to debrief about last week's prayer walk. Let them share what they saw and how God used that walk to show them needs in their town they perhaps had never noticed before. Then lead them in prayer, and have each person pray for the needs that have surfaced. Lead them in prayers of how their congregation may once again be strong and healthy in order to begin to address those needs.

THIRD SUNDAY OF THE MONTH

Creating Urgency: Just prior to the offering, show a brief DVD from a mission organization (such as World Vision or your denominational agency) about the desperate needs of another nation.

Casting Vision: As you prepare to take the offering, tell the people how the congregation will be taking a special offering next month to help meet some of the needs you have just witnessed on the DVD. Mention that this year's offering goal is 15 percent more than last year's offering. Tell them that you see a day when this congregation will not only double and triple their efforts in such offerings but will send teams to one of these nations to help people dig a well, build a building, etc.

THIRD TUESDAY OF THE MONTH

This is the night that you meet with Team Two (the vision team). Begin the meeting by giving a report of that which the prayer team discovered on its prayer walk and what that team has begun to pray in relation to the congregation. Begin to explore with them the needs they see in the town and perhaps the county. Remind them of the interview with the teacher, and get their feedback. Talk about how little the congregation will be able to raise to minister financially to those in a suffering nation or region of the world. Explore with them what some future strategies might be to begin to minister to these needs if the congregation were larger and had more human and financial resources.

THIRD SATURDAY OF THE MONTH

At 7 AM, meet again with your prayer team. Share with them some of the creative strategies that the dream team suggested to address needs in the community and around the world. Lead the team to pray that God will give you, the pastor, the wisdom to determine which of these strategies are from God and how to implement them. Lead them to pray that when these strategies are implemented, the congregation will embrace them. Lead them to pray that God will send the people and dollars to allow the congregation to implement these strategies with vigor.

FOURTH SUNDAY OF THE MONTH

Creating Urgency: Begin your sermon by sharing statistics about how irreligious our culture is becoming. Tell a story of how you were talking to a person in the community who did not have even a basic knowledge of spiritual things. Describe how many people have not been offered an understanding of Jesus Christ, God, and the Gospel. Show that most people in this community are hungry for spiritual things.

Casting Vision: In your sermon about Pentecost, describe how Jesus said that when the Holy Spirit came the disciples would be witnesses first in Jerusalem, then in Judea and Samaria, and then to the uttermost part of the earth. Talk about how two or three people in the congregation are embracing this concept by witnessing (telling what they know and have experienced) to others. Share how you are doing this at the gym where you work out. Declare that this congregation will one day be known as one where people individually and the congregation collectively are witnessing to God's love and saving grace. This congregation will not coerce or frighten with threats of fire and brimstone; rather, they will simply share what they know and have experienced with God. As a result, many people will come to Jesus just as they did at Pentecost. During the closing hymn, show a PowerPoint™ presentation with pictures of anonymous people. Title the presentation: Future disciples of Jesus Christ who were witnessed to by this congregation.

FOURTH TUESDAY OF THE MONTH

Meet with developing leaders (Team Three). Begin by telling them what the prayer team has learned this month, then share what the vision team is developing. Train these leaders about what vision is, how to cast it, and how it is related to urgency. Use your congregation and the things you are doing as examples. Teach them the difference between principles (overall concepts that work across cultures), strategies (larger designed plans to reach a particular culture), and tactics (specific plans that implement strategies). Talk about the principle of a healthy congregation and how that principle will one day be worked out in specific strategies and tactics in this congregation.

FOURTH SATURDAY OF THE MONTH

Meet again with your prayer team at 7 AM. Tell them that you have been training people in strategies and tactics. Have them pray for the strategy and the tactics that will make this congregation known for its witnessing. Have them pray that this congregation will again be filled with new disciples who have come because other disciples shared their knowledge of and experience with Jesus Christ.